WINGSPREAD

ALBERT B SIMPSON

WINGSPREAD

ALBERT B SIMPSON—A STUDY IN SPIRITUAL ALTITUDE

BY A W Tozer

CHRISTIAN PUBLICATIONS, INC.
Harrisburg, Pennsylvania

ISBN: 0-87509-218-7

Printed in U. S. A.

TABLE OF

Contents

Introduction

Any man who has reason to hope (or to fear) that someone may someday write the story of his life would do
well to pray that he may not fall into the hand of an
enemy, a disciple, a rival or a relative.

Of all men, these make the poorest biographers. Their
relationship to the subject places them where they cannot see him as he actually is, so the picture they paint,
however interesting it may be, is never true to the
original.

Our enemies seldom know us well enough to write
about us. The person they think they know—and hate—is
not the person we are. For that reason an enemy is likely
to draw a caricature, and not a true likeness. He is sure
to sketch in his prejudices and animosities, and may casually leave upon the forehead little careless projections
which could not be proved to be, but might easily be mistaken for, horns.

A disciple will usually do as poor a job, from an artistic point of view, as an enemy, though for an altogether

different reason. Instead of horns he may, with as little fidelity to the facts, sketch in a harp, but the result will be no better in the end. "Leave the warts in," said Lincoln when about to sit for his portrait, and to the everlasting credit of the artist he had the courage to do it. But true disciples never see warts, or if one is called to their attention, they will argue that it is only a callous anyway, caused by a halo that had slipped down.

George Washington has the misfortune to be respected by everybody and loved by nobody. Parson Weems saw to that. He wrote a life of Washington that fixed a great gulf between him and every downright American from that day forward. The pretty boy with the cherry cheeks, the innocent little hatchet and the sententious manner of speech which Weems gave to the world can never excite the affections of sincere men and women. But I wonder whether Lincoln's warts and his uncurried hair may not have created a secret bond of sympathy between him and two generations of American boys. No one wants a hero who is too perfect.

And where is that man who can write a fair biography of an acknowledged rival? It is not in human nature to do it. No matter how valiantly we may try, we cannot force ourselves to say all the good that ought to be said about a man when we know that every feather we put in his cap we must first take out of our own. That is why it is hard to get a fair appraisal of a public figure by a contemporary in his own field.

Our relatives know us better than anyone else does, but they are not safe biographers nevertheless. In the first place they are likely to be stone blind with pride and affection, (not to mention their uncomfortable habit of referring to us by little nicknames we hoped had been forgotten). The knowledge that one of their own blood and kin has actually attained to eminence acts like a draught of heady wine rendering them incapable of anything like sober judgment. By a well-known law of the human mind they praise themselves in their illustrious relative, so that what we get is a lot of left-handed boasting that does not come within shouting distance of the truth.

The best biographer comes from a far country. He can see the subject as he is, and being free from the handicap of a close personal relation, he will, if he have a fair amount of intelligence and enough patience to make himself familiar with the facts, be in a position to present a reasonably accurate picture of what he sees.

We feel that we bring to the task of writing this sketch of the life of Albert B. Simpson, if nothing more, a sympathetic heart and an objective mental approach. We belong to another generation than his, and thus stand back from the subject far enough to gain better perspective. We are not, and have never been his disciple, though common gratitude requires us to testify that we have received from his life and teachings, and more especially from his "spiritual songs," such immeasurable benefits that we feel forever bound to thank the thoughtful God who gave him to the Church. Meditation upon his trials and triumphs easily brings tears close to the surface and disposes us to reverent prayer. Indeed it is hard to write dispassionately of one possessing the tremendous emotional appeal of A. B. Simpson. The sheer spiritual

weight of the man crushes in upon us till we are over-
come with it and, like Daniel, we "sit down astonied." But
in spite of this, we shall try to maintain a fair objectivity
in our treatment of the subject matter which his life
affords.

In preparing this work we but loose his shoe latchet,
and acknowledge ourself blessed in the doing of it.

CHAPTER ONE

A child is born

The world's great men usually enter incognito. Emerson was wont to put his hand reverently upon the head of any urchin that might come his way. "Who knows," said he, "but I may be patting the head of a future president." The tough youngsters who gathered in Jesse's back yard of a summer afternoon to play the ancient equivalent of piggy-move-up would not have shoved Jesse's youngest boy around quite so freely if they had had a touch of second sight to let them see that they were taking liberties with the greatest king Israel was ever to know. But their blindness made possible many a glorious day of fun for the boys in the neighborhood, and it also guaranteed to David an uninhibited and normal childhood. Such are the ways of God when He prepares His saints and heroes: He leaves them unrecognized by the world until the day of their "showing unto Israel."

About all we know of the circumstances of the birth of little Albert Simpson is who his parents were, and that it was a bitter cold day the day that he was born. For he was born in Bayview, Prince Edward Island, Canada, December 15, 1843, and any day in December is cold on Prince Edward Island.

The plain, stove-heated room where was heard his first baby cry—that strange frightening sound, like nothing else in nature, and having no human quality about it —was made snug against the outside chill by the honest toil of the baby's father, hard-working James Simpson, the merchant, miller, and ship builder.

Jane Simpson, the mother heard that cry and smiled, and when they told her the child was a boy she may have wept a little, too, but her tears were tears of happiness, and not of sorrow. Her first baby had been a boy, and when he was just old enough to toddle over the floor and to say "mama" and "papa," he had died, and the light had gone out of her heart, and not even the presence of her other children, William Howard and Louisa, could bring it back again. So she had prayed that God might send her another son to take the place of the one who had gone, and her faith would have nothing less than that he become a minister or a missionary, though with good Scotch caution she had made her prayer plenty broad, "if the Lord so wills, and he lives to grow up, and is so inclined." It would not do to be too specific with the sovereign God, but, after all, He might listen to a suggestion.

And now what should the new boy be called? Well, plain James Simpson looked over his glasses and, with singular lack of imagination, announced quietly that he should be called Albert. James Albert had been the name of the lad who had died, but Albert was a good name,

12

and it saved a lot of thinking, so Albert it was. And the dutiful little wife agreed, and then timidly suggested that a second name be added, maybe a good Bible name such as Benjamin, if the father think it well. Perhaps she could not tell her husband why—that quiet, good man who worked every day, read heavy books on Calvinism, and had a reputation for great evenness of temper—but she remembered Jacob, and she treasured in her heart the hope that this boy should be her Benjamin, the son of her right hand. So it was settled, Albert Benjamin Simpson should be his name.

And when the neighbors gathered in to see the new lad, they must have remarked—with that friendly liberty we allow ourselves on such occasions—that the big noble-sounding name was pretty heavy for such a sweet wee mite to carry, and that if he lives a month with such a great fine name as that, he is as good as reared! And the mother's face shines with joy, and even the father allows himself a considered smile.

Right here we may as well see what history has been at long pains to teach us, that if you get a good mother it will not do to be too particular about your father; you cannot have everything. Give the boy a superior mother, and he will make the grade somehow. The women know this well enough, though they are not saying so in front of the men. Hannah looks down at the floor modestly and says nothing, but she searches for her own features in Samuel—and finds them there. And Manoah's wife, and the mother of Zebedee's children, and Monica, and Suzanna Wesley; what do all these teach us but the same thing every scientist knows, that greatness follows the maternal line? The men have impressive voices, they look knowing, and claim credit for every sign of intelligence in their offspring, but their masculine pride takes a terrible beating from biology.

There can be no doubt about it, Dr. A. B. Simpson, boy and man, can never be explained apart from his mother, Jane Clark Simpson. She gave him wings. Of a fine Scotch line she came, a line that could trace its history back to the old heroic days of Scotia's grandeur, of the persecutions, and the Covenanters and the fight to keep alive the faith once delivered. High strung and temperamental, with more than a dash of high romance, she had a soul too large for her small body. Straight from mother to son, following the laws of life, went this great soul, sensitive, poetic, beauty-loving, lofty. By the miracle of inheritance there appears again in him her ambitions, her aspirations, her soaring imagination. She had been accustomed to the refinements of the best society, and she never accepted the drab life of a Canadian farm wife as her own. A "guid wife" and mother she undoubtedly was to her unpoetic husband and her brood of boys and girls, but there were times when the dullness and monotony of her existence drove her almost to distraction. Then it was that her children, when she thought them fast asleep, would hear her sobbing out her disappointment and frustration long into the night. But these times were not many, and they seldom lasted long, for she had a mounting fancy, and she had her friends, and they would come to her even there in the ice-locked farm house. The poets, they were her friends, and she entertained them all, (except those wicked geniuses, which no

14

nice woman would read). But there were many good ones, Milton and Scott and Cowper and Dryden and Pope and Thompson; these and scores of others she loved, and to them she went for comfort when her heart was overwhelmed within her. Then she could dream her dreams, and live in fancy the life she had hoped to live, and be what she had wanted to be.

Not that James Simpson, the father, was not a good man. He most certainly was that. "Clean, capable, and industrious," they said he was, and religious, too. He probably had more religion than his temperamental little wife. Did he not pray every morning? And whip his children for laughing on the Sabbath? And believe in the shorter catechism and the five-point star of Calvinism? But imagination he had not. And poetry? Well, it was to be tolerated, and especially the metrical psalter was good, but he was busy, and after his daily portion of Baxter's *Saint's Rest* and Doddridge's *Rise and Progress*, he had little time left for poetry. But he was a kindly man and only looked mildly amused when he came in of an evening and found his wife nursing the baby with Milton's *Complete Works* propped up in front of her. He lived a quiet life and did well by his family, and was an elder in the Presbyterian Church for half a lifetime. Louise Simpson, writing at a very advanced age, recalls that there was "sunshine" in her father's life, but Albert apparently saw little of it, and the picture he presents of his father is certainly not marked by sunshine. Albert remembers something else much more vividly; severe discipline, those endless Sunday afternoon drills in the catechism which began with the philosophical poser, "What is the chief end of

15

man?" and concluded twenty-four pages and 105 questions later with, "What doth the conclusion of the Lord's Prayer teach us?" That was the shorter catechism, but not a boy or girl standing in line in the dimly lighted parlor of the Simpson farmhouse while the sun shone soft on the flowers outside would believe there was anything "shorter" about it.

CHAPTER TWO

As the twig is bent

And the child grew, and his mother stole many an admiring glance at him, for she saw that he was a proper child, and his sweet, tender face, with great shining eyes that reminded people of Shelley, was good for a mother to look upon. But religion must come first, and the Simpson household was nothing if not religious. The parents had set themselves to bring up their children after the manner of their Scottish forbears. Sharp discipline, stern rules, severe restraint upon conduct, all these young Albert knew, with big chunks of theology which he confessed later he could not understand, crammed into his head daily. Then there was church, family prayer, the catechism, and long dry books by the reforming fathers, more prayer, and church again. Strange it is that in the midst of all these religious calisthenics no one remembered to tell the sensitive, eager boy how to be saved. The love that gave all, even life itself, for its enemies, was tragically overlooked in the boy's education, and it nearly proved to be the undoing of him.

2

While the rigorous religious training which the boy received did not bring him to a state of grace it did instill into his impressionable young mind the all-importance of religion to the race of men. By the time he was ten he already had a secret yearning to become a minister, and while still short of his teens he was struggling with the idea, desiring to be a minister, but unwilling to pay the price. The preachers he knew in those days must have been a dour and artificial lot, for the sum of his testimony is that he wrestled with himself over the question of whether to become a minister or to flee the service of the church and remain a human being. After several rounds with death when the old Leveler came so close that the boy felt his cold breath on the back of his neck he finally decided to renounce his humanity—and he felt that it would mean nothing less than that—and preach the Gospel. Duty dictated this, and it is to his credit, and to the everlasting honor of his parents, that he could muster enough courage to make his decision to "do right though the heavens fall." Imperfect as it all was and as tragically lacking in the accents of grace it yet revealed a heart that was feeling after God, and more than all it showed that God had not forgotten Jane Simpson's timid request, "that the boy might be a minister or missionary, if he live to grow up, and is so inclined," nor yet the impassioned prayer of inspired John Geddie, the Apostle to the South Seas, who had baptized the lad and dedicated him to the ministry shortly after he was born.

So are the ways of God with men. The facts are there to prove it, no matter how our sleek orthodoxy may kick against the pricks—Albert Simpson was called to the ministry before he was converted, and God said of him, "I have even called thee by thy name though thou hast not known me." If God could—and would—ordain Jeremiah to the ministry before he was born, then he could call Albert Simpson to preach, the lad being yet unregenerated—and he did just that. As far as the boy was concerned he would preach the Gospel somehow, that was settled for him.

About this time James Simpson called one of those painful family councils where solemnity is so thick you can cut it with a knife and the atmosphere is heavy with a wholesome chastening misery, and with the wife and mother sitting by proceeded to charge his two pre-adolescent sons with their respective duties and to map out their future for them. He was a good man, a product of his times and a faithful son of his stern religion, and he is not to be censured that he did not know a swan when one appeared among his brood of ducklings. David's father had made the same mistake, had tried to push every son he had under the prophet's oil except the one whom God had chosen. Howard, the eldest son, is to prepare to enter the ministry, and Albert is to stay at home on the farm and help with the chores! If the good man had only crossed his arms like Jacob he would have been right in his decisions, but he failed to do so, and was one-hundred percent wrong. The blindness that would hang up such genius as young Albert's along with his torn straw hat on the wall of the farm kitchen is too deep and dismal to excite anything but pity. But we have all done as badly at some time; we have all failed to recognize the prophet behind his disguise, so modesty dictates that

19

we pass over this mighty error with no cocksure comment.

Even at that tender age the boy had pretty well learned to discipline his feelings, so apart from a few impulsive and eloquent gulps, he made no remonstrance as his father pronounced the words that meant the end of all his secret hopes. Then a glance at his mother and courage comes to him: He rises and stands respectfully before his father with clasped hands and, with "broken words and stammering tongue," he pleads for permission to enter the ministry, provided he can get his education at his own cost and make all necessary preparation, with no expense to the family exchequer. It must have been a moving plea, for it took something to unmake the made-up mind of a Scotch Presbyterian elder. When the boy is done and has sunk down exhausted into his chair, his father rises, stands a moment to get control of his voice, and then in trembling tones gives his consent and a "God bless you, my boy." So it is finished. The boy will be a minister. God has willed it and the lad is so inclined.

CHAPTER THREE

Out of the paw of the lion

His determination to enter the ministry never left the boy, and we see him at fourteen, physically weak, but possessing a mind far beyond his years, studying Latin, Greek and higher mathematics under a private teacher, as a step in the direction of his goal. But the stripling was attempting the impossible. Remember that up to this time he had had no satisfying experience of grace, and he was trying to do as a son of Adam what can only be done by a son of God. He was preparing for a ministry in the Spirit, and his troubled heart told him that he was yet in the flesh. And temperamentally he was at cross purposes with himself by his very nature and upbringing. No matter how hard his intellect tries it cannot keep up with his racing soul, his soaring imagination. Already the poet and the theologian are at war within him; John Keats and John Calvin are having it out to the finish, and young Albert is both of them, taking a brutal slugging no matter which one wins. His teachers have tried hard to make him into a good, solid, logical young man,

21

staid and conventional, with his two feet firm on the hard ground; but nature will not work along with them. She will be forever singing to him, forever tempting him away from the sullen earth and bidding him stretch his wings to the blue heaven.

When just short of fifteen he leaves his private teacher and enrolls in Chatham High School, which is located nine miles from the Simpson home. Of course, this necessitates a daily trip of eighteen miles through all kinds of weather—and they have all kinds in that part of Canada. He rode a horse as often as one could be spared from necessary work on the farm, but it seems that he still had to commute on foot more frequently than a boy of fifteen should have done, especially one of his delicate constitution.

Now that other mysterious change begins to take place. The trusting boy is passing away and the seeing man is emerging, first the one and then the other taking the ascendency. Physical maladjustments add themselves to the temperamental conflict already raging within him. Hard study has weakened his nerves and predisposed him toward despair. Suddenly the accumulated terrors of a multitude of books and sermons on total depravity and the damnation of the non-elect roar out upon him like a lion from the thicket and throw him into mortal panic for his dying soul. He cries out in anguish, but there is no one to help him. The proud man within him will not permit him to go to his mother with his fears, and the timid boy dare not go to his father. How can a boy talk to a somber Presbyterian elder about anything as painfully intimate as that, especially when that elder is your father, and you remember how solemn and awful your father used to look at you when you missed one question in the catechism or smiled on the holy Sabbath? And you remember how he used to sentence you to a whipping in the evening, and then wait till morning to carry out the sentence; and you can still feel the cold chill that would come over you when you woke for the hundredth time in the night, and at last saw gray light which you shuddered to think was the herald of the dawn, and the trouncing.

Well, the human organism can take only so much, and the distressed boy had had enough. Suddenly came that "fearful crash," of which he later wrote so movingly, when the very heavens seemed to be coming undone before his terrified eyes; a blazing light shines above him, and his familiar earth crumbles away from beneath his feet, plunging him down into the center of spinning worlds and crashing ruin. He comes out of this physical spin only to go into a worse mental spin a second later. He leaps up in mortal agony and stands impaled upon the point of a fixed idea like a fly upon the point of a pin; he is to die in a few minutes, when that clock there on the table is on the hour, and it is four minutes of the hour now! Any help will do at this moment. His pride and fear give way before a greater terror, and he cries aloud for his father to come and pray for him. The father does not fail him. Beneath an exterior of cultivated austerity is a great Scotch heart, full of tenderest affection. His boy is dearer to him than "the ruddy drops that visit his sad heart." It may be a bit irregular, and he cannot just remember where such a thing is found in the

Scriptures, but father love overcomes doctrinal objections, so down he goes to his knees to pour out his heart for his darling lad with all the strength there is in him. God has mercy on them both, and the boy is able to relax a little, though for days he cannot sleep unless someone is near to assure him, and he will go into nervous spasms as the fatal hour approaches—the torture hour fixed like a sharp stake in his exhausted mind—and will hardly believe he is alive when the hour has passed. And still no one could tell him the simple gospel story. Strange no one remembered the story of the prodigal boy and the kind, trembling old father who received him back again from the far country with the touching, tender words: "For this my son was dead, and is alive again; he was lost, and is found." Such is the power of loveless doctrine to freeze the heart and dull the mind. So the stripling had to struggle back to health again as best he could without the consolations of divine forgiveness.

Well, as God would have it, when he had recovered enough to be about again, though still in terrible distress for his soul, he was one day browsing among the books in his old minister's library when, all unexpectedly, the big moment came for which he had waited so long. He flipped a page in an old musty volume, called Marshall's *Gospel Mystery of Sanctification,* and suddenly his eyes were fixed on a passage that stood out like fire from the rest: "The first good work you will ever perform is to believe on the Lord Jesus Christ. Until you do this, all your works, prayers, tears, and good resolutions are vain. To believe on the Lord Jesus Christ is to believe that He saves you according to His Word, that He receives and

saves you here and now, for He has said: 'Him that com-
eth to me I will in no wise cast out.'" That was enough.
A heart as hungry as his and a mind as keen, needed no
more. With rapture he slid to his knees and closed with
the promise, and there came to his soul such a sweet,
restful knowledge of sins forgiven as swept away his fears
like a flood.

God had delivered him out of the paw of the lion.

CHAPTER FOUR

He chooses smooth stones

It is significant as well as amusing to see how many Biblical prophets kept sheep before assuming their prophetic office, and how many modern prophets taught school. The schoolhouse has been the vestibule to the church house for a multitude of successful ministers. And it was so with Albert Simpson. He knew he needed the money and God knew he needed the experience, so when only sixteen and looking much younger, he sat with boyish dignity and drilled into a room full of over-age students from the Canadian prairies the fundamentals of education. Some of these students were nearly twice his age, and yet they obeyed him like lambs. He wondered why, and with characteristic modesty fails to see that they are but paying tribute to his inherent gift of leadership. They felt something—and none of them could have told what it was—that made them want to follow that intelligent, self-assured youngster. Their instinct was sound; he was a born leader, and with his ability to influence the masses he could have been a dangerous man if he had fallen into other ways than the ways of God.

During these days of teaching and study his spiritual life grew like grass by the water courses. His testimony at this time abounds with phrases that show how the stripling was thriving in his new life of faith: "The promises of God burst upon my soul with a new and marvelous light. The glowing promises of Isaiah and Jeremiah were clothed with a glory that no tongue can express." He must have literally devoured the Scriptures, and with what he calls "unspeakable ecstacy" he marked his favorite passages. No giant has appeared as yet, but with fine spiritual intuition he is choosing smooth stones from the brook. He will need them later on.

At seventeen he decides—as a result of reading again his father's old favorite, Doddridge—to confirm his spiritual experience by a solemn covenant, God, as the party of the first part, and himself, as party of the second part, being the high contracting parties. The dead seriousness of the boy is apparent here. He sets aside a whole day for fasting and prayer, and then at the close of the day draws up and signs and seals the covenant.

This covenant is one of the most remarkable things produced by any boy-Christian in any period of the Church's history. Artificial and stilted in language it admittedly is, but back of the old-fashioned language and borrowed mode of speech a great soul is discoverable. The covenant itself runs into about nine-hundred words, and follows an unconscious parallel with a Sunday morning service in the Presbyterian Church in Chatham or any other town of that day.

It begins with the Sunday morning prayer, "O Thou everlasting and almighty God, Ruler of the universe,

Thou who madest this world and me Thy creature upon it, Thou who art in every place beholding the evil and the good, Thou seest me at this time and knowest all my thoughts." A little later comes the hymn, where he says he would,

> *"Come before Thee as a sinner*
> *Lost and ruined by the fall."*

From there he launches into a Calvinistic sermon that would have warmed the heart of any Scotch Covenanter, but that no boy would ever have thought of by himself: "Thou, O Lord, didst make Adam holy and happy, and gavest him ability to maintain his state." (From a boy of seventeen!) "The penalty of his disobedience was death, but he disobeyed Thy holy law and incurred that penalty, and I, as a descendent from him, have inherited this depravity and this penalty. I acknowledge the justness of Thy sentence, O Lord, and would bow in submission before Thee." Several "points" are developed in the same vein, and then he announces the closing hymn.

> *"I am now a soldier of the cross,*
> *A follower of the lamb."*

After that comes the benediction, "Now give me Thy Spirit and Thy protection in my heart at all times, and then I shall drink of the rivers of salvation, lie down by still waters, and be infinitely happy in the favor of God."

This "covenant" is done, of course, in ordinary prose, but the music is in the background plain enough to be heard by any keen ear. The whole thing is an astonishing piece of work, revealing a remarkable familiarity with the

Scriptures for a boy of seventeen, and evidencing a psychology entirely dominated by the Church. It is a solemn and beautiful song in the creation of which Paul and Calvin collaborated on the words, and King David wrote the music.

In all this—his school teaching, his eager study, his religious vows and spiritual adventures—there is seen a dual purpose leading him on. There was the over-all purpose of God, of which the boy was but dimly conscious, weaving in every thread of providential circumstance to make a mantle for this prophet; and there was the firm conscious purpose of the boy himself. For there was something sweetly deceptive about this smiling gentle youth. Underneath his mild exterior there lay a will like an iron beam. He had a purpose in his heart that completely controlled him. Once he had settled his call to the ministry this mighty purpose took over and drove him like a benignant master for the rest of his days. If ever there was a man who knew why he was alive that man was A. B. Simpson. He is preparing to answer the old question, "What is the chief end of man?" in deeds as well as in words. No other kind of answer would do for that kind of man.

CHAPTER FIVE

He leaps over a wall

The news that "Brother Simpson's son, Albert" had been called to the ministry got around pretty fast up Chatham way and out among the country folk in Kent County, Ontario. But the aspiring prophet soon learns that a call from God is not sufficient; he must secure the approval of the senior prophets of the Presbytery before he can hope to make his voice heard in any Presbyterian pulpit in the land; and that approval is not an easy thing to obtain. The Presbyterian Church of that day had built a wall around its pulpit too high for any but the most heroic to leap over, and what is a green country boy to do?

The sponsorship of the highly respected Rev. William Walker, and the reputation of the boy's father, James Simpson, the elder, brought him to the attention of the proper church authorities, so in the fall of the year 1861, while still two months short of his eighteenth birthday, he appears with a number of other candidates before the formidable and awe-inspiring Presbytery at London, Ontario. After sitting in silence for several hours, during which time they were studiously ignored by the members of that august body, they are subjected to an examination that singes their pride and roots out any traces of conceit that might have survived that long siege of letting alone they had endured earlier in the day. The members of the examining board undoubtedly were one and all men of genuine Christian principles, and it is not hard to believe that they must have had good hearts about them somewhere, but this was no time to be soft, so they proceeded to take the boys apart piece by piece to see what made them run, and they examined the "parts" to see whether they were the stuff of which ministers are made.

We smile with sympathy for the country boy as he stands before his judges, and we could wish that they had been a bit less exacting in their demands, but in the light of the history of Protestant Christianity on the North American Continent over the last hundred years we cannot but admit the stern wisdom of their actions. If the men of that day erred it was on the side of right, and their error was inspired by a lofty conception of the sacredness and dignity of the Christian ministry. The wave of amateurism that swept over the American pulpit a generation ago with such tragic results would not have been possible if the Christian churches had maintained a higher standard of requirements for the ministers of the sanctuary. Protestantism has been in the Book of Judges for three-quarters of a century, where "every man does that which is right in his own eyes," and the evil consequences are beyond computing.

Well, that class of candidates must have been a well instructed lot, for they passed their examinations without

31

any casualties, and were all recommended by the Presbytery for admission to Knox College to study for the regular ministry.

In less than a month after this Albert Simpson entered Knox College, Toronto, and began his course of studies there. From the first day it was apparent that a youth of unusual powers was among them. Whenever he arose to speak the eyes of everyone were upon him. Speaking came as easy to him as singing to a bird. As a preacher, he was a "natural"; he never had to learn how.

The friends back home have been hearing good things of the boy away there in the big city. They know that he is a lad of parts, a keen and knowing lad who will go far in the learned world; but can he preach? That is the question these friends are asking. It was hoped that young Albert would prove to be a good speaker as well as a brainy student, but these cautious Scotch neighbors were not doing any wishful thinking. They would wait and hear for themselves.

When the Christmas holidays came around and it was known that the young man was coming back for a short vacation the interest ran so high that the church at Tilbury, near his home, arranged to have him preach at a Sunday morning service. A prophet hath no honor in his own country and among his own people, and who are these that crowd the little church that Sabbath morning but his own neighbors and kin folk? The skeptical are there, and the curious, and the whole Simpson family is there, all sitting in a row, hoping desperately that he may do well by himself, but getting braced for the shock in case he forgets his place and breaks down.

When the vestry door opens and the preacher walks in the silence is so deep the worshipers can hear each other breathe. There is many a suppressed smile as he takes his place in the pulpit, for he is but a youth, and ruddy, and of a fair countenance. At the proper moment the boy preacher rises, announces a text and launches into his carefully memorized sermon. He is soon speaking without effort, speaking not with his rich musical voice alone, but with his whole graceful body, every part of him alive and in tune with the melody of his words. It is a great sermon, an unbelievably great sermon for a youth of eighteen. For orthodoxy it is blameless, for clarity and logic it is of the first order, and for beauty and effectiveness of delivery it beats anything these old sermon lovers have heard for many a long day. After this there is no more doubt about Brother Simpson's son, Albert. He has proved his right to the prophet's mantle. These stoical listeners say nothing, but they bless him with their eyes and adopt him with their hearts; they are proud of him. The boy is not only smart, he is a natural born preacher as well, a little young yet, but mighty good to listen to.

Reputations are hard to make among people such as these, but once made they travel far and fast. After that first sermon at Tilbury Albert Simpson had no trouble to get a hearing. Preachers were never too plentiful anyway, and preachers of the caliber of this young man were rare indeed, so there came to him many invitations to preach in churches large and small.

Back at college, Albert studied hard and made rapid progress—if indeed it is accurate to say that a young man studied hard who literally ate up his subjects without trying. He was gifted with such superb mental equipment as made anything like real grinding study unnecessary. The ease with which he carried forward his studies made it possible for him to accept quite a number of preaching engagements throughout the school year. This meant a bit of financial assistance—badly needed we may be sure —and it meant also opportunity to gain increased skill in the exercise of the art to which he was born, the art of the public speaker.

His fame as a boy preacher—just turned eighteen when he first came to public notice, and looking much younger—spread throughout the churches, but in spite of all they had heard of his extreme youth the steady-going Presbyterian congregations were seldom prepared to receive such a mere boy into their pulpits when he arrived to preach of a Sabbath morning. The good Scotch elders wrestled long with their scruples when they were compelled to hand the huge old pulpit Bible to this handsome stripling before the service could begin. They did na' like it at a', though for the life of them they could not tell what rule the lad was breaking being so "unco" young. But seeing that he had been sent out by the seminary there was nothing to do but swallow their fears and allow the service to proceed. And when the service was ended their qualms had given way to cautious smiles, as bright as becomes men in the hoos o' God who are nevertheless mighty well pleased with the way things have turned out.

With the financial aid he received from his family plus the small amounts he could earn as supply preacher here and there and an occasional windfall in the form of a small scholarship earned in competitive examinations he managed to stay on in college until he had completed the required work. In April, 1865, he was graduated from Knox College. It must have been a big day for him, for in some sense it was the last payment on the promise he had made to his parents there in the parlor of the old farmhouse that memorable afternoon when he had humbly begged permission to enter the ministry and preach the Gospel provided he could manage to secure the necessary education.

The regular education he received did, without doubt, contribute much to the total of his greatness as a man and as a minister of Christ, but it did not in any sense make him what he was. Indeed he wore his collegiate honors lightly, accepting them casually and by the way. He was always bigger than his books. Happily for the church he was too much of an individualist to take the academic stamp. Saul's armor was an interesting thing to have around, and maybe occasionally to try on for size, but when he went out after giants he asked for nothing more than his sling and five smooth stones from the brook.

Two months after graduation from Knox College Mr. Simpson was called to appear with a number of other candidates before the Presbytery at Toronto for examination with a view to their being licensed as ministers of the Canada Presbyterian Church. They called the examination "public probationary trial" and they tried to live up to the name. They went over the minds of these young men with a fine comb and searched their hearts with a candle. Biblical Hebrew and Greek, Theology, Church

History and Church Government: The examiners would find out how much the candidates knew about these subjects (and they must know a great deal or they would be rejected). After that they were subjected to a searching examination concerning their personal religious experience. That they had already given proof of the genuineness of their spiritual experience as a necessary qualification for their admission to Knox College did not matter. Those old-time Christian scholars knew what they wanted, and they believed they knew what God wanted. They were not going to license an ignoramus or a sinner if they could help it. And they thought they could. So there followed a number of tough papers of various kinds to be prepared and read before the Presbytery, including a Latin thesis, an excursus, a popular sermon and a lecture, all given in cold blood as *samples*. It is not recorded that they also performed a sample marriage ceremony and baptized a baby, but we would not be too much surprised if we discovered that they did.

Anyway everything turned out for the best, and in due time Albert Simpson was licensed to the Presbyterian ministry. He has cleared the barrier. He is a minister at last.

CHAPTER SIX

He feeds his father's sheep

Knox Church, Hamilton, was one of the finer churches of Canada, very well-to-do and respectable, with more than twenty years of colorful history behind it, having a large congregation, and equipment the best that money could buy. It had a reputation among the churches, and when for any reason its pulpit became vacant the greatest preachers of the Presbyterian ministry were called to fill it. Such are the ways of churches. The ones that have, to them shall be given, and they shall have more abundantly, and the largest churches take it for granted that they should be able to command the biggest preachers. And ministers, being still human, are too often ready to agree with them.

In the summer of 1865 the pulpit of Knox Church was left vacant by the resignation of the brilliant Dr. Robert Irving, and a call was extended to A. B. Simpson to become the new pastor. Here was news indeed and material for a world of small talk among the church people and the ministers as they gathered here and there for the

Monday autopsies. True, young Simpson is an eloquent speaker and bright as they come, but after all he is only twenty-one years old and without pastoral experience; and Knox Church is one of the most important in the whole Dominion of Canada. Its pastors have been of the cream of the Presbyterian ministry. They have established a tradition for brilliancy in the pulpit next to impossible to maintain, altogether impossible for a mere boy just out of school. So went the friendly gossip. And it is easy to believe that the boy from the farm near Chatham, Ontario, was willing to admit that there might be some truth in it.

About this time a small church in the little town of Dundas, Ontario, also extended Mr. Simpson a call to become its pastor. A drowsy delightful little hamlet was Dundas, made up of respectable, well-to-do people who were pretty well satisfied with themselves and not much given to overdoing their spiritual activities. Yet they were a religious people, too, and maintained a quaint and sleepy little church which they loved and attended once or twice a week without fail. They had heard the eloquent young Simpson while he had been still a student at Knox College, and, knowing a rising star when they saw one, they wanted him for their pastor.

This complicated things for the young man. Years later he tells of the confusion that was in his mind over the problem before him. Ambition said, take the large church. Morbid humility said, take the small one. Like Solomon the young preacher was being tested here, though he knew nothing of it at the time. If he had been just one inch shorter in spiritual stature he would have taken the small church to keep himself humble, or he would have taken the large one to satisfy his ambition. But being who and what he was, he sat down and reasoned like this: If I take the small church it will demand little, and I will give little. Result, stagnation; I will get soft and cease to grow. If I take the large church I will be compelled to rise to meet its heavier demands, and the very effort will develop the gifts of God which are in me. The small church may break me; the large church will certainly help to make me. So he notified Knox Church that he would accept.

Now, A. B. Simpson, for all his humility, had a flair for the dramatic. He loved to surround himself with a multitude of activities, to do things in a big way. So he planned a gala week for himself, to be replete with events so important that any one of them might have been enough to fill a week for the average man. But A. B. Simpson was not the average man. So on September 11 he delivered his maiden sermon as the new pastor of Knox Church, Hamilton. The next day in the afternoon he appeared before some of the local luminaries and was solemnly ordained to the ministry by prayer and the laying on of hands. That same night he caught a train for Toronto, and the next day he was married! Then followed a short honeymoon trip down the St. Lawrence, a swift journey back across the country to Hamilton and a rousing reception for the bride and groom given at the manse by the members of Knox Church.

He is four years away from the farm, and three months out of school, but he is already the pastor of a large city church, an ordained minister and—a married man!

The woman who became his wife was Margaret Henry, daughter of an influential elder in Dr. Jenning's Church in Toronto. They had been acquainted for about four years and had been engaged for the better part of that time. Temperamentally, Margaret was the exact opposite of her sensitive, poetic husband, and there is reason to believe that she never quite fully understood him. Until his death, more than fifty years later, he continued to be something of a puzzle to her. She did not always sympathize with his religious convictions, but for more than half a century she remained a faithful wife to him, devoting herself unselfishly to the care of their family of six children. In her later years she became a very earnest Christian worker, and proved to be a real help to her husband in his public ministry.

Mr. Simpson remained with Knox Church eight years, and enjoyed an eminently successful ministry throughout the entire time. The figures show that he actually added to the church during that time a total of 750 members—and all without the aid of evangelistic meetings or any other special efforts; he did not believe in them!—paid off an indebtedness of $5,000 on the church property, organized a Woman's Aid Society (the grandmother of all Alliance Prayer Bands), started a number of prayer meetings within the program of church activities, and sparked his people on to such fervent missionary giving as they had not dreamed possible.

What he was able to do for Knox Church is of interest to a considerable few, but what Knox Church and the grace of God did for him during those years is of far greater importance to the whole Church of God and the

40

work of Christian missions. He began his work there a boyish looking young man just short of twenty-two, possessing tremendous capacities, but still untried and undeveloped. He left that church eight years later a mature, experienced, traveled minister of wide reputation, in constant demand as a preacher and lecturer both in Canada and in the United States.

A photograph taken toward the close of his Hamilton pastorate shows an impressive looking—if somewhat camera-conscious—clergyman, intelligence written all over his handsome countenance, dressed in a long black robe done with many shirrs and pleats, and with a white ascot hanging from his chin eight inches down over his bosom. It is of interest to observe that the plague of baldness had attacked him early, for even at that time there are unmistakable evidences that his hair had started to go. He resembles somewhat the Rev. Charles G. Finney at that age, only a bit less self-assurance, and a whole world more of worry in those troubled eyes. And the worried look is not imaginary. It had good reason for being there. The man had not yet come out into the sunlight. The eagle was still chained to the hard earth, but he had begun to catch sight of blue patches above the mountains and he heard within him the call of the heights, a call to which he did not yet know how to respond. The look of mild distress is seen on most of his pictures until the crisis experience that brought the Holy Spirit into his life in joyous fullness; after that it is seen no more, but falls away like the scales from the eyes of Saul.

Two years before the termination of his Hamilton ministry his church generously granted him a four-month

41

furlough and sent him to Europe. This trip is of little interest to us now, for it must be admitted that the fashionable young clergyman went simply because it was the custom for really big ministers to see Europe or the Holy Land, or both. In the days before the earth had shrunk to the size of an orange and any small town Babbit might "do" Europe, it was a grand thing for a preacher to go abroad. The prestige it gave him was worth a year's salary at least. Any chance member who had the temerity to disagree with the minister after that, could be quickly set in his place with the effective squelch, "Why, our minister has been abro-ad!" And the minister himself could squirm out of many a tight spot in his sermon by clearing his throat impressively and saying, "When I was abro-ad lawst time." Verily all things have their uses.

CHAPTER SEVEN

He takes a short flight

After eight years with Knox Church Mr. Simpson began to feel a stirring toward a new field of labor. Calls were coming to him from many places in both Canada and the United States. One such interested him particularly, a call to become the pastor of the large and important Chestnut Street Church in Louisville, Kentucky.

No one who knows even a little of the life and labors of A. B. Simpson can fail to see that God was here going ahead of him to make the way straight before his face, but it is true nevertheless that certain motives entered into his decision to accept the pastorate of the Louisville church that do not appear to be directly spiritual. God was answering his heart's yearning for "better things," but He was compelled by the very nature of the man to lead him by such means as He could find in the circumstances. We do Mr. Simpson no favor by insisting on reading into his life (and especially at this stage of his development) a degree of spiritual perfection which he himself did not claim. In the first place, his health was suffering from the effects of the harsh climate of Ontario, and a change to some region where milder weather prevailed would be a welcome relief to the flesh. Then the salary of $5,000 per year offered by the Chestnut Street Church looked mighty good to a harried young husband with a wife possessed of expensive tastes, and a family of six to support. Add to this the further fact that Louisville was a much larger city than Hamilton, affording almost limitless opportunities to a wide-awake minister, and it is not hard to see how attractive the proposition looked. He decided to move to Louisville.

He resigned from the pastorate of Knox Church, Hamilton, about the middle of December, 1873, and began his work in Louisville the early part of January, 1874. It may be of no consequence and hardly worth mentioning, but it is at least a curious fact that Mr. Simpson's life revolved around the fall and winter season as the Dipper around the North Star. He was born December 15 and died October 29. He was married in the middle of September, and took his first pastorate also at that time. Each change of pastorate was made around the time of the winter holidays, and so far as we can learn nearly every spiritual crisis came to him and almost every major life decision was made by him at the cold season of the year. Was there something in the constitution of this winter-born organism that reached its highest peak of aliveness when the sun was low down in the sky and the winds blew chill? Science may some day answer a question like that. As yet we can only wonder, and turn away without reply.

Chestnut Street Church belonged to the Presbyterian

Church North, which, a traveler from another planet might be shocked to learn, means this: that years after the Civil War had been lost and won, and Grant had clicked his heels and handed back to Lee his officer's sword as a generous gesture toward a gallant but defeated foe; after the silver-lipped Grady had come north from Atlanta and thrown his arms around both the North and the South and hugged them close together in that great oratorical classic, "The Old South and the New"; after Lincoln had gone down in blood to the immense sorrow of a whole united people; after the gray-clad soldiers had put down their guns and gone back to raising sweet potatoes on the river bottoms of Georgia and Tennessee; after the senators from down south were back in Washington holding forth on the glory of southern manhood and the virtues of southern fried chicken, and getting applause from the galleries, and the country was getting back to normal again, *the churches were still fighting the Civil War*. The world fights and forgets; God's people fight and remember.

The bitterness between the churches—even churches of the same denomination, distinguished only by that pugnacious countersign, "North" or "South"—was chilling the religious life of those cities lying near the line of Mason and Dixon, and freezing every sporadic attempt at revival put forth by any of them. Louisville was a northern city in a southern state, or a southern city in a northern state (depending upon which way you hold your map, and whom you are talking to) and the smouldering animosity between the churches was particularly marked there. The new pastor of Chestnut Street Church

45

felt this the moment he arrived. At first it lay like a heavy burden upon his soul, but gradually he began to sense that he had been called to Louisville for just such a time as this. Here was he, a neutral Canadian from far up beyond the Yankee frontier. He could not possibly have any Civil War feeling one way or the other. The people sensed this and the prejudices of both factions were set at rest. They accepted him simply as a gifted and eloquent minister of the Presbyterian Church—no odious geographical directions included—and they were ready to listen to him. Here was his opportunity, and he did not fail it.

After a few months of surveying the field and getting acquainted he launched his quiet campaign of reconciliation. He sent out a call to all the pastors of all denominations in the city of Louisville to meet in the Chestnut Street Church to consider a matter of vital importance to the spiritual life of the city. When they had assembled he laid before them a plan to hold a city-wide union revival campaign for all the churches at some central auditorium, and appealed to the pastors present to get behind the effort. Then, knowing that if they were permitted to start talking they would talk their bristles up and the meeting down, he suggested that they now get on their knees and call upon God for revival. It worked. Down they went, that crowd of preachers, and the first stage of the campaign was won. As they prayed the fire grew so hot that everyone was melted except one old die-hard who ground his teeth shut, scooped up his hat and stalked out for keeps. It was a fine thing. The others had gotten such a spiritual uplift that they were ready to bring the

Civil War to a close without further bloodshed and get down to the business of winning men to Christ. Amid tears and smiles and handclasps that crowd of happy preachers sat down to plan their winter revival.

They had their big names in that day even as we have in ours and as they had in the days of John the Baptist, names that had about them a magic power to draw the crowds and focus public attention. Among the greatest was Major Whittle, a tender personality with mighty pulpit gifts and a consuming passion for the souls of men. Him the pastors of Louisville secured for their winter campaign. The meetings were held in Public Library Hall, a huge auditorium in the heart of the city. There, night after night for weeks, upward of two thousand people from every level of society from the gutter to the colonial mansion gathered to hear the message of life. Whittle preached and P. P. Bliss sang. The city was moved to its depths and hundreds were converted. At the close of the campaign large numbers were received into the churches, scores joining Chestnut Street Church, the church which had taken such an active part in the revival campaign.

The success of this campaign was a revelation to Mr. Simpson. Up to this time he had been very much of a church man, visualizing the whole religious picture as an adventure in respectability. The minister would be doing what he once called with much dignity "the regular work of the ministry," serving all who came within the sphere of his proper interest, but stooping to nothing novel, nothing that would in any way compromise the godly gravity of the cloth. He had been willing to slave his heart out within the proper framework of approved church activities, but, like Peter, he had been such a child of his ecclesiastical upbringing, that he needed a special revelation to make him see that people were dearer to God than forms, that the "lesser breeds without the law" were the objects of God's present love and anxious care more than all the rules and regulations of the Presbytery. Though it had been his vision that brought the meetings to the city, the meetings themselves so greatly enlarged that vision that A. B. Simpson was never the same again. He had become—though he did not yet realize it fully— an evangelist to the masses. The cry of the millions was coming to him, the bleat of the other lost sheep. From here on he belongs no more to one church, but to all who need him, not to his parish only, but to all the lost world.

However, a spiritual preparation was necessary in the life of A. B. Simpson before his dream of world-evangelism could be realized. It is remarkable how great a man can be, how faithfully he can labor in the gospel ministry, how much, indeed, he can appear to accomplish in the work of the church, and still be far short of the rich, power-driven service possible to the Spirit-filled servants of God. Mr. Simpson began to see this plainly, and the knowledge was not comforting to him. Until he came into contact with Major Whittle he had not realized how much of pride and self there was within him, and how little of the power of Christ. As he listened night after night to the preaching of the great evangelist a vast uneasiness came over his heart; the hyphenated self-qualities, self-love, self-confidence, self-seeking, all that Adam-begotten brood of illegitimate soul children which inhabited his life, began to make him sick utterly. There was something about Whittle, some overtone of power, some fragrance of Christ, some hovering Presence that melted the brilliant young Presbyterian minister like a vision of God. A thousand flaws appeared to him, galling, painful, Christ-dishonoring; and worst of all a constant gnawing emptiness within him, a desperate sense of spiritual suffocation. He must have more of God. He must be filled with the Spirit.

It was characteristic of the man that he must settle everything with God alone. From the first he had been a lone eagle. Others could inspire him, could help to create spiritual desire within him, but when the crisis came it would be—indeed, for him, it *must* be—when he was shut in with God in lonely wrestling like Jacob by the side of Jabbok. His struggle was wholly internal. Outwardly he was the same poised, gifted and highly respected minister of the church, but inwardly he felt himself a dying man, forsaken and alone. The time appears to have been some days after the close of the Whittle meetings. There in the privacy of his own room, with not one soul to understand or to sympathize, his Gethsemane came to him; old Adam stood on him and weighed him down till he was crushed as olives are crushed in a press. He yielded himself to God in utter surrender, "Not knowing," he says, "but it would be death in the most literal sense before the morning light." And death it was in a most literal sense too, but death to the old man, to the old self-asserting ego. God accepted his offering and blessed him in a degree he had never known before, had hardly dared to dream possible. From that hour he was turned into another man. He would live from that time on, in his own words, "a consecrated, crucified, and Christ-devoted life."

All that happened that night is known only to God and A. B. Simpson. Indeed it is doubtful whether Mr. Simpson himself knew the full implications of that mighty work of dying he accomplished there in the divine Presence. But things were different after that. The eagle had broken loose and was stretching his wings. It was a great triumph in the Spirit, and was prophetic of lofty flights to come.

CHAPTER EIGHT

The humble hear a voice

Whatever others might do Mr. Simpson could not settle back to follow the prescribed duties of a pastor, and nothing more. He must evangelize. It was in his blood now and nothing could stop him. He suggested to the pastors of Louisville that work which had started under Major Whittle be continued every winter by the churches of the city uniting in a great Sunday evening evangelistic campaign to be held in Public Library Hall. They were sympathetic with his zeal but they were not prepared to give up the security of the regular Sunday evening services to which they had been so long accustomed. For one campaign of a few weeks yes, but every year, and for long periods, well, you see, it would interfere with the habits of good church people and work a hardship on the local treasuries. Then it did smack of religious excitement, of enthusiasm a little out of hand; everything should be done decently and in order. On the whole they felt it would not be wise to agree to such a proposal, so they voted no, and the proposition was rejected.

Rev. A. B. Simpson, pastor of Chestnut Street Church, would not be stopped by the cautious, if kindly, arguments of his brethen in the ministry. There was a lot in what they said, to be sure, but what was it all and what did it amount to when set over against the terrible fact that thousands walked the streets of Louisville who were without any hope of salvation, and who would be forever without that hope if the churches continued on in their regular groove? They had not reached these thousands, and just now they had voted not even to try to reach them.

Mr. Simpson called his people together and laid the matter before them. The new blood circulating through their veins had come like a transfusion. They had come to like the sight of new converts and the sound of fresh testimonies. They were ready to hear their pastor. In a few weeks the Sunday evening meetings were discontinued at Chestnut Street Church, and the whole congregation went in a body to Public Library Hall for their evening services. The news spread like fire, and soon the auditorium was packed with men and women of every sort from all Louisville and vicinity. Simpson preached the Gospel to lost sinners with a tender grace unknown to him before, and unknown to most of the church people who heard him. He appealed directly to the hearts of the people and made no bones about it. They were lost, God loved them, Christ had died for them and now invited them to come home. They ought to come at once, no delaying, no waiting. He accepted as a foregone conclusion the truth of Christianity and refused to turn from his ministry of reconciliation to engage in argument with the

52

half-persuaded or the unbelieving. What mattered one objection to the seven-day creation period, or a dozen objections to the inspiration of the Scriptures for that matter, or any other objections, when one hundred people were waiting to turn to God as soon as the way was explained to them? He was familiar with religious polemics, but he was too wise to engage in it before a congregation of lost men. So he went directly to the people's hearts and sought to win them to Christ by any means that lay within his power.

The daily papers took up the story of the Sunday evening evangelistic effort and gave it first page publicity. It may be that they were fed up on church dignity and relished a glimpse of simple humanity in the pulpit, or it may be that as newsmen they recognized a good story, but whatever the reason, they adopted Mr. Simpson and his Sunday evening meetings as an object of particular attention. Every Monday his sermon of the day before— at least a large part of it—appeared in the Louisville papers. No amount of paid advertising could have done as much as this did to boost the attendance. Indeed the attendance was no problem; frequently the problem was to find room for the crowds that flocked to the services.

Mr. Simpson had learned from Whittle and Bliss the value of good gospel music. The crowds that came each Sunday night to Public Library Hall heard music, lots of it, the best that could be obtained; they enjoyed vocal combinations of every sort from solos to a chorus choir, and they joined in mass singing of old time church favorites and the more recent Gospel songs, composed by Sankey, Bliss, Crosby and others of the gospel musicians

of the day. Popular? Sure it was popular, and it was
frowned on by many of the sterile scribes of the syna-
gogues, but to Mr. Simpson the word "popular" carried
no terrors. It meant "of the people," and it was people
he was interested in. The dignity of the clergy could take
care of itself; it would never lack defenders, but the
people, the sinful, friendly, seeking multitudes: they mattered more than the opinion of some austere guardian of
decadent orthodoxy. So the singing went on and the
crowds loved it and kept coming back week after week
to enjoy it.

The heart of A. B. Simpson was delighted with what
his eyes were beholding. He felt more than ever that this
was to be his work. The scales were falling away and he
was beginning to see clearly. The old idea of a little flock
fed and comforted and bedded down for the night without a thought of the lost ones out of the wilds became
unbearable to him. He must evangelize. His church must
be an evangelistic church first and everything else only
after it had done its work of evangelization. And now he
comes forward with a brand new plan and lays it before
his people. It is to build in the center of the city a plain
but commodious tabernacle, built not after conventional
church lines, but for utility, and located where the
crowded ways cross each other, where the rag tag and
the outcast, the poor and him that hath no helper may
feel free to come and never worry because their clothes
are ragged and out of fashion; where the common man
with his middle-class wife and large family can come and
not be uneasy if the baby makes a bit of a disturbance
during the service. In short he proposes that his church

become a center of evangelism for the whole city; that it change its psychology and think no more of its reputation, but rather of the lost of Louisville. Chestnut Street Church was already well out along that path and needed little prodding. With the exception of a few who could not see it, and left the fellowship, the members agreed to the radical step. A lot was purchased and the work of building begun.

The winter following, Chestnut Street Church sought again to obtain Public Library Hall for their Sunday evening meetings, but found the way blocked. There was a little politician in the wood pile somewhere and the city authorities would not rent the hall. The new tabernacle was still in process of building; the Sunday evening mass meetings must go on. Result, the daring Mr. Simpson went straight to the owner of Macauley's Theatre and requested the use of the theatre (one of the largest and most popular amusement centers in downtown Louisville at that time) for Sunday evening services. It must have been a bit of a surprise to the gentleman who owned the theatre, for he was too painfully aware of the low esteem in which he and his worldly business were held by the church people. But business is business and the deal was made.

When opening night rolled around and the multitudes flocked to the theatre to a religious service, there was a rending and splintering sound heard throughout all the churches: it was the wholesale smashing of religious precedents by Chestnut Street Church and her lovable but over zealous pastor! Many a stiff and proper saint that

55

night drew his robes close to him and wondered in hollow tones what Christianity was coming to. This was carrying things too far! Nothing good could come of it!

We who live nearly three-quarters of a century removed from those times may find it hard to understand why there should have been any objection to the holding of gospel meetings in a theatre. The explanation is simply that we have had two generations to get used to such meetings and it was new to them. We are no broader, no brighter than they were; we merely have custom on our side, and they had custom against them. We have seen it done before, and they had not. On such a matter as this, religious people do not think anyway, they merely react. Their emotions decide the verdict, and any thinking they may do is of very low wattage, and is brought in mostly to support their prejudices.

Now, after we have discounted the objector's reasons ninety-five percent as pure rationalization of religious taboo-reaction, there still remains something to be said in favor of his position. Worldly plays are given in the theatre every night; irreligious and unwashed actors and actresses speak their profane lines, sing their spicy songs and dance their suggestive dances to the great delight of the graceless mobs that attend. The place, then, must be bad, altogether bad, and no child of God should go in the theatre. It cheapens the Gospel to take it to a theatre; it lowers the prestige of the Christian religion to go to a place of worldly amusement to pray. This was the line of attack on the meetings, and it sounded pretty convincing to the staid church people who wanted to be convinced.

The newspapers (which had no inhibitions about the

56

matter) defended Mr. Simpson against these critical attacks, and a few church leaders came to his side of the controversy, but the "best" people remained irrevocably opposed to such low-brow goings on. As for the pastor and his people, they smiled and went their way. They knew the answers. A place is good or bad, said they, depending upon who is in it and what they are doing. Things are never bad in themselves; they are merely neutral, becoming bad or good only as they are used for purposes either right or wrong. The theatre itself—the floors and walls and seats—is not bad *per se,* and when a crowd of people enters it bound on a holy errand, it becomes good, better than any consecrated shrine could be where men approach it in loveless duty or unbelief. And as for the prestige of the church: they had never heard that a shepherd loses prestige by going out into the mountains to bring the wandering sheep back to the fold again.

The new tabernacle went up slowly and—as is often true—the cost went up rapidly. What had started out to be a modest building costing about $65,000 was blown up by the mounting ambitions of the trustees into a magnificent edifice running well over $100,000. About half of this was subscribed; the rest was church debt. Mr. Simpson fought this to a standstill, but the people won. He had fired their zeal, and now he was unable to direct it. He had wanted a plain building, tailor-made for the uses of mass evangelism, but low in cost and out of debt. They had given him a beautiful and imposing structure comparing favorably in appearance with the finest buildings in the country, but in debt to the tune of nearly $50,000.

The new building—to be called Broadway Tabernacle —was at last ready for occupancy, and the Chestnut Street Church people moved in and went to work. But there was no dedication. Mr. Simpson flatly refused to dedicate debt. He made no effort to hide his feelings. "Church debts," he told the people grimly at the opening service, "are properly called *church bonds,* and a church with bonds is not free." At the conclusion of his sermon he called upon his people to rise in one brave, final sacrifice and clear off the debt then and there. "This morning," he cried dramatically, "I desire to place on this pulpit the simple standard, Broadway Tabernacle Free! free from debt, free to God, free to all." But the good people of the congregation were not equal to the occasion. They just could not muster heroism enough to meet the challenge, and the debt was allowed to remain.

For the two years that Mr. Simpson remained in Louisville after the erection of Broadway Tabernacle he continued to preach to the multitudes that crowded in to hear the message of salvation. The dream of his heart was being fulfilled; Louisville was hearing the Gospel and hundreds were turning to God. But a shadow remained over the tabernacle and over the heart of the pastor—the ugly shadow of debt—and he was not completely happy even though there were unmistakable evidences of God's favor upon the work.

For those who like to toy with the riddles of history we record the following fact: A year after Mr. Simpson had left Broadway Tabernacle, and only about three years after the structure was built, the indebtedness was suddenly and unexpectedly paid out in full. Two months later the building went up in a roaring fire that destroyed it completely! All this presents a tangle of divine providence and inscrutable purpose too badly snarled for me to unravel. Anyone can work on it who has the time.

CHAPTER NINE

This dreamer cometh

God had found a man after His own heart, a man too
great to keep shut up in one parish or in one city. The
world would be his parish, as Wesley had phrased it, and
A. B. Simpson was beginning to sense his high destiny.
Yet there can be little doubt that Mr. Simpson, at this
point in his life, was as unaware of the great career that
lay before him as Moses had been at the burning bush.
He kept hearing "a strange and secret whisper like a
dream of night that told him he was on enchanted
ground." There remained within him still a strong love
for the established church, a wish to carry out his large
purposes while yet continuing to serve his denomination.
It is no reflection on that honored body that he could
not do it.

He was walking softly, seeing only a little way ahead,
letting each providential step explain the one preceding
it. Unknown to him he was taking the prescribed way of
the gospel witness, "Jerusalem, Judæa, Samaria and the
uttermost parts of the earth." Hamilton had been his

Jerusalem for eight years; his Judæa had been Louisville, and now he is feeling himself stirred to move on to Samaria. From there it would be "the uttermost parts" in a degree known to few men in the history of the Christian Church. But he did not know this yet. He did know one thing, however: the call of the unevangelized was upon his heart. He felt a strong tug toward some larger field of service; maybe it would be New York, he was not sure, but he wanted to get near to a center of missionary activities, and New York looked like the place.

To some extent Mr. Simpson had always been interested in foreign missions. His father had been a warm friend of the missionary cause and he had heard missions talked around the table as early as he could remember. While still a mere boy he had been stirred to the depths of his heart by the story of Rev. John Williams, the missionary martyr, and he had wanted then to become a missionary. All through the years there had been times when he felt, or imagined he felt, the holy hand of John Geddies upon his brow. He had been too young to remember that scene there at his baptism when the great Apostle to the Islands had dedicated him to God, but his mother had never let him forget the fact or the circumstances, and the knowledge of it remained as a charge and a benediction.

The new missionary impulse felt currently among the churches on both sides of the Atlantic, personal contacts with missionary minded Christians, and, above all the new anointing which he had received from God sharpened up his missionary interest till it glowed like a hot point. A world of reasons, of information, of practical missionary truth broke around him, sweeping away apathy, answering every objection and *compelling* him to be a missionary. And still he would not say "yes." It was the way of this God-possessed dreamer. His call must come direct from the Throne. Logic would not do. Reasons were not enough. There must be a spiritual experience concerning the matter or there would be no response.

So one night he lay down to sleep, not consciously thinking about the lost world, but subconsciously very much troubled. By intellectual conviction he was a missionary, but he was not satisfied. Everything was so human yet, so mental, so much a matter of texts and statistics. It was all only half-way down in his heart. But he was waiting, and suddenly it happened. "I was awakened from sleep," he says, "trembling with a strange and solemn sense of God's overshadowing power, and on my soul was burning the remembrance of a strange dream through which I had that moment come. It seemed to me that I was sitting in a vast auditorium and millions of people were sitting around me. All the Christians in the world seemed to be there, and on the platform was a great multitude of faces and forms. They seemed to be mostly Chinese. They were not speaking, but in mute anguish were wringing their hands, and their faces wore an expression I can never forget. As I woke with that vision on my mind, I trembled with the Holy Spirit, and I threw myself on my knees and every fiber in my being answered, 'Yes, Lord, I will go.'"

When the Book of the Chronicles of the Holy Ghost is written, that night will mark the beginning of a new chapter, for then was born a movement which has proved to be one of the greatest missionary agencies of modern times. A missionary *must* had come to a Spirit-filled man, a man big enough to do something about it, a man great enough to make himself heard to the farthest corners of the earth. The cold-hearted will frown on the words "vision" and "dream," the timid will wonder, the psychologist will look interested, reach for his book on abnormal psychology, and leaf over to the section that treats on religious delusions, and smile knowingly. But the years tell another story.

A. B. Simpson had become a world-missionary, whatever men may think of it, and he had come through in the only way a man of his temperament could. For better or for worse that was the way he moved. He would first get an idea, a concept, then must come a heart experience to set it off, to detonate the charge it contained. Until the explosion came, he could wait, sometimes for years, mulling his idea over, half forgetting it, burying it under a mountain of work; then the great day would come and he would be prostrated, almost slain under the impact of that idea, his and yet God's idea, leaping up now, and powerfully compelling as it came out at him like a blast of creative force.

To the earth-walking Christian, ankle-deep in dust, who has never seen heaven opened or beheld a vision of God, this will seem all out of order, too emotional, too extreme. But it is the way of the strong eagles of the kingdom, the prophets, the apostles, the reformers and revivalists. These fly high and see far, and that they are not understood is no great wonder. The sky-loving eagle, screaming in the sun, may be a puzzle to the contented biddy scratching in the yard, but that is no good argument against the eagle.

The years, I say, tell their own story. Nowhere else in the field of human endeavor can so little pass for so much with so many as in religion. It affords unlimited opportunity for men to rise like a rocket—and come down like the stick. And the catch is that those who saw the pseudo-Moses go up are seldom around when he comes down, so no one notices it anyway. But time puts the correct price tag on everything.

The true test of spiritual greatness is permanence. By this test A. B. Simpson stands triumphant. It is now sixty-seven years since he dreamed his dream of world-evangelization, and fifty-six years since was formed the society that arose at his call to give realization to that dream. The work he founded has stood up under the strain of two world wars and three major economic depressions, and is going stronger with each passing year. It has lived through how many moral revolutions in society, philosophical about-faces in learned circles, shifts in theology among the churches and radical changes in religious methods everywhere? Yet the work goes on, turning not to the right hand nor to the left, its original vision undimmed and its initial purpose unaltered.

The early months of the year 1879 were important months in the life of A. B. Simpson. His world-call was becoming stronger, and his plans were beginning to take shape. He was getting more confident now, surer that his vision was from God, that the "uttermost parts of the earth" were to constitute his field of service. His dream of multitudes, "in mute anguish, wringing their hands," was slowly interpreting itself to him, making itself plain, and he was not forgetting his promise, "Yes, Lord, I will go."

To dream, in the language of Mr. Simpson, was not to sit in pleasant reverie within some ivory tower mercifully apart from the harsh realities of the world. Rather it was to reconnoiter, to search out the strength and position of the foe, to decide strategy and to mass for the attack.

Not that there had been no other dreamers before him, no others who had caught a vision of world-evangelization. Indeed, the work of foreign missions had lately come into greater notice than at any time for centuries gone. There was quite a stirring among the dry bones in those days; a respectable army of missionaries had stood up out of the dust of generations of neglect of the Great Commission. God was laying sinews upon them, putting breath into them, and they were going to hitherto forgotten parts of the earth with the message of Christ. But their numbers were small and their efforts were scattered; the field was wide and, at its best, the interest among the churches was slight. Something was being done, to be sure, but it was only as a drop of rain now and then on a thirsty desert, to be instantly, eagerly swallowed up and lost in the parched vastness that was heathenism. A new all-out effort was needed, a wider dissemination of missionary information, a magazine— yes, that would be it, a magazine to promote the work of missions. Mr. Simpson saw it now like a flash of light. He would launch a new kind of magazine, one devoted wholly to the cause of world-missions, a digest of missionary news, full of reports of work accomplished, interesting descriptions of conditions among the heathen, a challenge to the churches, and a call. And why not get into step with the modern trend toward pictures and illustrations? It would be different, but that would be in its favor. Yes, he would illustrate his new magazine with the newest type wood cuts, and maybe, later, engravings made from actual photographs taken on the trail. Then the people could *see*, as well as read about the tribes and tongues and peoples to whom the Gospel must be sent.

To carry out this plan it would be necessary for him to be close to some center of missionary operations, some port from which missionaries sailed, and to which they returned again brimming over with missionary enthusiasm. There was just one such city in the United States; he was sure of it now. It would be New York. He must locate in New York where he could see and interview men and women who knew the fields, who could furnish fresh information to make his magazine live. The various denominational boards stayed mostly each within its own little half-acre; the work of one did not greatly help the others. Denominational barriers interfered. What was needed was a journal that could serve as a clearing house for missionary news of all the churches, that could toss the fire across the fences and spread it everywhere. His heart glowed with the thought of what might be done. But Louisville was not the city from which could be launched such an ambitious undertaking. The good people of Chestnut Street Church, for all their evangelistic zeal and their love for the lost, were not ready to follow their pastor in his vision of world-missions. He must find more favorable surroundings.

Then suddenly the way was plain before him. A call came from New York. Dr. Burchard was leaving the Thirteenth Street Church, and the church officers were sure that no one but A. B. Simpson would do as his successor. He had preached there some time before and was no stranger to the people. The call that came was cordial and urgent. Would he come? And at once? It did not take him long to put two and two together. An urge from within and a call from without: He immediately resigned his Louisville charge and moved on to his new field in the city of New York, beginning his work there in November, 1879.

The arrival of the new pastor marked a sharp upturn in the life and activities of Thirteenth Street Church. A new spiritual impulse was evident at once. The people were revived; church attendance increased rapidly; many were converted and numbers were added to the church. As the months went on everything looked good to the church officers, mighty good, if the pastor would only stick to his parish and not show so much interest in the poor and the lost of the city streets. Certainly someone had to labor for their salvation, but not the pastor of fashionable Thirteenth Street Church. That church was not a rescue mission. They hoped the pastor would keep that in mind. Its members were well-to-do people, fairly along toward the top of the social ladder. They were real Christians, and they would support any project as long as it was for the strengthening of their own church. They welcomed any new member who was of their own kind.

67

But after all, the church is the church, and it must be protected from the—well, inelegant influences of the commoner classes.

Mr. Simpson sensed their attitude, but he did not quite know what to make of it. His vision was bigger than one church, his love deeper than one social stratum. He wanted his church to give up its narrow exclusiveness and become a center for the evangelization of the masses. The church officers could not see this. Definitely, Thirteenth Street Church had its traditions to maintain and its prestige to protect. They watched the pastor with considerable uneasiness, though for the time being they spoke gently and kept their anxiety to themselves; they dare not risk losing such a giant from their pulpit. He was young, and besides he was from the west. He would learn.

But when, one day, the pastor came before the session and asked permission to bring into the church upwards of a hundred converts from the Italian quarter, which he had won while preaching on the streets down in the poor neighborhoods, they felt the time had come to lay upon the young man a firm but kindly hand. They were more than pleased, they explained, that those poor Italians had been won to Christ, but did the pastor think they should come into *their* fellowship? They would not be the social equals of the rest of the members, and would likely not feel at home anyway. Could he not find a spiritual home for them among others of their own kind? Mr. Simpson said he thought he could (and he subsequently did), but this experience opened his eyes to the futility of trying to carry out his plans through the medium of a regular church—at least that church. He accepted the rebuff graciously, but he began to dream again, and his dream did not include Thirteenth Street Church.

CHAPTER TEN

The shadow declineth

When he had been in New York only a little more than a year Mr. Simpson's labors were suddenly interrupted by a break in his health so serious as to force him to quit all pastoral duties, as he then thought, for good. He had never been robust. At fourteen years of age he had been brought near to death when his whole nervous system went into complete collapse. A few years later, during his first pastorate, and while still a very young man, he had suffered another physical breakdown so severe that he was compelled to drop all activities and rest for a period of weeks. During much of the time he had been at Louisville he had labored under the handicap of painful physical infirmities. "I labored on for years," he declared, "with the aid of constant remedies and preventives. God knows how many hundred times in my earlier ministry when preaching in my pulpit or ministering beside a grave it seemed that I must fall in the midst of the service or drop into the open grave." Now the strain of his many activities in New York had done its evil work. The old trouble of heart and nerves came back upon him with increased terror. So grave was his condition this time that a prominent physician told him frankly that his days were numbered.

Along with brain weariness and weakness of nerves and body came a heavy visitation of gloom, totally depressing all his powers and plunging him into a Slough of Despond so deep that further work was impossible. He secured a leave of absence from his church and left for the health resort at Saratoga Springs to try to recruit his wasted powers. But nothing helped much. "I wandered about," he later wrote in describing his experience, "deeply depressed. All things in life looked dark and withered." And that from a man who had told of spiritual joys and ecstasies and high flights into the realms of love and bliss. So it was, and so it is; and once more the low-flying Christian will find it hard to understand.

This work is trying to be what it set out to be; no defense, no uncritical eulogy, but a fair and frank portrayal of a man whose common human nature made him subject to all the temptations flesh is cursed with, and who yet deserves to be studied as a thrilling example of what the grace of God can do for and through human weakness. A. B. Simpson needs no gloss from us; he is well able to stand on his own legs; his place in modern church history is secure.

Nevertheless, to sharpen our focus somewhat and bring our picture into better perspective, we point out that Mr. Simpson's conflict with Giant Despair was nothing unusual in one of his temperament. On those occasional descents which he admittedly made into the nether regions, those Dantean visits through the dark forest and into the blind world, he was not alone. The company he shared on those painful journeys (if he could but have remembered it) was probably far better than that he left behind him. For the great had traveled that way. David had wandered there sometimes, his voiceless harp under his arm, all its strings hanging broken and mute; Jeremiah had been often there, and the rough stones of the way had been damp with his tears; even the mighty Elijah had spent a little while in the shadowy vale in full retreat—we wince to admit—from an angry woman; Luther had gone at least once down the dark road and—as if to balance accounts—had been led by a woman back into the sunshine again.

It is characteristic of the God-intoxicated, the dreamers and mystics of the Kingdom, that their flight-range is greater than that of other men. Their ability to sweep upward to unbelievable heights of spiritual transport is equaled only by their sad power to descend, to sit in dazed dejection by the River Chebar or to startle the night watches with their lonely grief. A long list of names could be appended here to support this statement; and it would be a noble and saintly list indeed, for Moses' name would be there, and Thomas Upham's and Brother Lawrence's, and St. Francis', and Madam Guyon's and a host of others. It might well read like a little Who's Who in the Kingdom of God, if the whole truth were told of the gloom of the great, which overtakes them sometimes on their journey to the City of God.

While at Saratoga Springs Mr. Simpson chanced to stroll out to a religious meeting at a near-by camp ground. He was not greatly impressed with what he saw and heard till a Negro quartette stood up and sang what has now come to be known as a "spiritual." It was one of those single-string affairs, carrying but one idea, and repeating that idea over and over, English round style, till the end of the song and the bottom of the page were reached:

"My Jesus is the Lord of Lords:
No man can work like Him."

It was not much, but it was enough. It took nothing more artistic than a braying ass to rebuke the madness of a prophet, and the crowing of a barnyard cock turned the feet of an apostle back into the narrow way. So it came to pass that a simple "spiritual" was used of God to lift a future world-missionary from despair.

There is a compensating feature about the mystic temperament: that is its quick pick-up, its astonishing ability to take off from a standing start. That quaint Negro song acted like a catapult to launch A. B. Simpson into the air. "It fell upon me," he said later, "like a spell. It fascinated me. It seemed like a voice from heaven. It possessed my whole being. I took Him also to be *my* Lord of Lords, and to work for *me*. I knew not how much it all meant; but I took Him in the dark, and went forth from that rude, old-fashioned service, remembering nothing else, but strangely lifted up." *Strangely lifted up:* there you have it, the language of deliverance, the voice from the heights. This was not imagination; it was real. The wounded eagle had found his wings again and was soaring back into the sun.

Only slightly improved physically, but now altogether out from under the spiritual cloud, he returned to New York to take up his pastoral duties again. But there was no use telling himself that he could carry on; he was clearly a sick man. The physician's prediction seemed to be on its way to fulfilment. The shadow was declining. It looked as if his sun was about to go down while it was still day.

There was every reason why Mr. Simpson should desire to live. His family needed him. Two daughters there were, and three sons, the eldest boy being still in his early teens and the youngest girl a mere baby. And he loved these noisy youngsters, did their father, with an overflowing tenderness of devotion possible only to one of his torrid emotional nature. To leave them now, and to leave their none-too-robust mother with the burden of their upbringing! It was more than he could bear. And the call of the lost world, the unevangelized masses who might never hear the Gospel if he failed them, what could he do about these? What about the magazine, and the "Yes, Lord" which he had said to foreign missions, had repeated as a bride repeats "I do" at the altar? And the multitudes "in mute anguish wringing their hands?" The high ambitious plans and the long dreams, what of these?

It was a trusting, but confused and frustrated minister who would walk slowly, painfully about the streets of New York during those summer evenings, old, tired and through—at thirty-seven.

CHAPTER ELEVEN

He finds the fountain of youth

The year was 1881. Throughout the Protestant world there was the sound of a going in the top of the mulberry trees, strange stirrings and motions of spiritual life, felt everywhere, but more distinctly noticed in independent fellowships and outside the sacred precincts of conventional Christianity. Laymen were awaking to the work which the clergy had been neglecting. The Salvation Army, a laymen's movement, had been founded in London some years before by "General" William Booth, and was getting off to a running start in most of the great cities of the English-speaking world. It was the church of the humble, the army of the outcast and the friendless, but it had power, and with that disconcerting persistence of all movements that are *born* rather than merely organized, it knew where it was going and was on its way. The Holiness Movement, a renaissance of John Wesley Methodism with a few additions of its own, was just coming into notice in this country. Dwight L. Moody, the converted shoe clerk, was traveling up and

down the country swaying thousands with his blunt un-
adorned eloquence, and winning hundreds of converts
wherever he appeared. His success was encouraging
other gifted soul winners to launch out into huge cam-
paigns of evangelism. Rescue missions were springing up
in all of the larger cities; street meetings were common,
and religious parades, all equipped with uniforms, brass
bands and drum majors, were becoming familiar sights
in many places.

Taking it all in all things were moving in gospel circles. America was responding to the urgings of the Holy
Ghost, but her response must be after her own genius
and in a manner characteristic of the rough and robust
spirit of a generation whose fathers had conquered a
continent.

Out of the creative spiritual yearnings of those times
was born a religious phenomenon, fathered by doctrine
which, though never wholly approved by the guardians
of formal orthodoxy, has nevertheless been loved by
countless eminent saints of every shade of theological
thought within the framework of evangelical Christianity
from Paul's day to the present time. We refer to the doctrine of divine healing. The sovereignty of God over the
human body was being recognized by some reputable
Bible teachers, and the privilege of the believer to take
his sicknesses to God in prayer with expectation of relief
was being taught by increasing numbers both in Europe
and in the United States. Reports of supernatural heal-
ings were coming from widely separated parts of the
world. Pastor Blumhardt in Germany, with his triumphant battle cry, "Jesus Is Victor!" was having amazing

success in praying for the sick. Dr. W. E. Boardman in England, and Dr. Charles Cullis in the United States were seeing remarkable cures wrought in answer to be-lieving prayer. Many less prominent persons were going quietly about their mission of mercy, praying the sick back to health, and humbly refusing to allow their names or their persons to be advertised.

No effort to understand the life and work of A. B. Simpson from this point on can be a complete success if we overlook the part played by Dr. Charles Cullis, the Boston physician. Dr. Cullis had been for some time head of a tuberculosis sanatorium in the city of Boston. His sympathies were deeply stirred by the distress and hope-lessness of many of his patients, and being a sincere Christian he was moved to pray for their deliverance. There followed recoveries so speedy and unusual as to hint of the miraculous. Soon he discontinued the use of other means and sought to bring his patients back to nor-mal health through the prayer of faith alone. The outcome was that he became convinced of the scripturalness of this method, and began to teach it as a Bible doctrine. He soon gave up his medical practice and went into full-time Christian work, preaching from place to place and praying with the sick. His work became widely known and many flocked to him for spiritual and physical help.

In the summer of 1881 Mr. Simpson visited Old Orchard, Maine, a famous summer resort and convention ground on the Atlantic Ocean. Heart and nerves had failed him. He moved about slowly in great weakness and bodily pain. Dr. Cullis was conducting a gospel meeting in an amphitheatre near the ocean side, and Mr.

Simpson felt a desire to attend. In these meetings he experienced another of the great crises of his life, one of such revolutionizing character that it may be said that his real world ministry began there. All before had been preliminary.

At the Cullis meetings he heard men and women testify to supernatural healing. His own great need compelled him to give close attention to these testimonies. Not the sermons, mind you, nor the eloquence of the evangelist, nor the earnestness of the appeal, but the witness of those who had been healed. "I heard a great number of people testify that they had been healed by simply trusting the word of Christ, just as they would for salvation."

Here was a sail on the horizon! A light, however dim, in the darkness! With that fine co-ordination of head and heart which always marked the man he went to work on the data before him. Those who testified, he reasoned, had no motive for misrepresenting the facts. They stood to gain nothing by their witness. All evil motive was ruled out. Of course, they could be mistaken, but two facts there were which could not be hurdled on that hypothesis: They had been ill, that was the first one. They now stood upon their feet completely sound, that was the second. They believed the Lord Himself had touched them and delivered them from their afflictions. If they could be healed, why could not he? He was beginning to hope.

However, common sense advised caution. With all of his propensity for quick intuition and swift flight he was a Scotsman still, a son of canny James Simpson who had to be convinced. He would not be taken in by the enthusiasm of these well-intentioned people. He must know for himself. "It drove me to my Bible," he testified. "I am so glad I did not go to man. At His feet alone, with my Bible open, and with no one to help or guide me, I became convinced that this was part of Christ's glorious Gospel for a sinful and suffering world, for all who would believe and receive His word."

He was running true to form. He now had a conviction, he had discovered a doctrine, but he must have spiritual confirmation or he could not go on. Reason was not enough. He must meet God and *experience* the power of the doctrine. The Spirit must furnish evidence that he understood the Scripture aright, that he was not mistaken in his position. So one Friday afternoon he walked out under the open sky, painfully, slowly, for he was always weak and out of breath in those days. A path into a pine wood invited him like an open door into a cathedral. There on a carpet of soft pine needles, with a fallen log for an altar, while the wind through the trees played an organ voluntary, he knelt and sought the face of his God.

Suddenly the power of Christ came upon him. It seemed as if God Himself was beside him, around him, filling all the fragrant sanctuary with the glory of His presence. "Every fiber in my soul," he said afterwards, "was tingling with the sense of God's presence." Stretching his hands toward the green vaulted ceiling he took upon himself the vow that saved him from an early grave, and—as subsequent developments revealed—changed the entire direction of his ministry and made him the greatest exponent of divine healing that the Church has seen in a thousand years. Preacher that he was his vow must be divided into "points," three in all, and they summed up his faith in the Word and his willingness to trust it forever. "It was so glorious to believe," he said, and he made this vow: 1. He would solemnly accept the truth of divine healing as a part of the Word of God and of the Gospel of Christ. 2. He would take the Lord Jesus as his physical life, for all the needs of his body until all his life-work was done. 3. He solemnly promised to *use* this blessing for the glory of God and the good of others. All this he earnestly pledged himself to do, as he put it with trembling awful devotion, "as I shall meet Thee in that day."

He left that piny temple a man physically transformed. A few days later he went on a long hike into the country, did this weakling minister for whom the grave had been eagerly waiting, *and climbed a mountain three thousand feet high.* "When I reached the mountain top," he relates joyfully, "I seemed to be at the gate of heaven, and the world of weakness and fear was lying at my feet. From that time I have had a new heart in this breast." The old trouble never visited him again.

Facts are glorious, tough, stubborn things, and they are fine criteria against which to measure our beliefs. Wesley taught that any doctrine which was found untenable in practice should come under suspicion of being erroneous and should be carefully re-examined in the light of Scripture. If it would not *work* in real life it was not likely to be the true teaching of the Bible. The converse is also true. Here was a man, weak and broken and hardly able to get about, who discovered in the Scriptures what he took to be a doctrine of hope for the physical body. He could be wrong. But he trusts it and becomes instantly and completely well. That may not be conclusive evidence of the correctness of the doctrine, but it is presumptive evidence of sufficient weight to deserve respectful consideration from every honest investigator.

Mr. Simpson soon found that he could not enjoy his new life unmolested. Many who had had no interest whatsoever in the thin sickly young minister so long as he was sickly and thin, leaped forward at once to protest his healing now that he was sound and well again. They assailed him for his belief that God will heal the body, and brought forward unanswerable arguments to show that He will do exactly nothing of the kind.

None of these objections did Mr. Simpson try to answer. He needed no arguments. He had something infinitely better. He had abounding, overflowing health, and he had it with hardly an interruption for the next thirty-five years. Before his healing he had looked so frail as to excite pity. After that experience there in the pine woods he took on much weight and looked the picture of vibrant health. Furthermore, he had found the secret of sustained health, of taking physical strength from the Lord day by day as he took oxygen from the atmosphere. And it was no fancy religious notion. For half a lifetime after this he was enabled to do a work so enormous as to stagger belief. Indeed I can think of none except Paul and Wesley who compare with him for quantity of work turned out. Year after year he kept at his mighty task, with hardly a day out for rest or recreation, up to within a few months of his death. These are stout tenacious facts. They are hard to circumvent. Whatever our beliefs may be the facts are there challenging us, demanding to be explained. Maybe Mr. Simpson's explanation is as good as any: "I do not desire to provoke argument, but I give my humble testimony, and to me it is very real and very wonderful: I know it is the Lord."

In all candor, it must be said that not all who opposed him belonged to the scribes and Pharisees. Many men of unquestioned sincerity and genuine Christian character took issue with him. And it cannot be denied that as the years went by much of the criticism he suffered was invited by his persistent support of the doctrine of divine life for the body. For he did not forget point three of his vow there in the pine woods. He would *use* the truth of healing to bless mankind. For the rest of his life he preached divine healing. Always he subordinated it to the greater truth of salvation through the blood of Christ, but always he kept the charge he felt had been committed to him for the suffering bodies of men.

Whether he would or not the name of A. B. Simpson and the doctrine of divine healing were wedded for life. The Irish have a proverb, "Whoever marries a mountainy woman marries the mountain." Mr. Simpson soon learned that in embracing divine healing he had opened his arms to all of its relatives, good and bad, for all time, past and present. The disadvantages went with the blessings. Every believer in the doctrine was forced to carry the odium of every fanatical excess which might have been practiced in the name of healing since the dim dawn and abysm of time. Mr. Simpson was not so naive as to be surprised by this. He rather expected it, but it hurt him, nonetheless. He never enjoyed being a martyr. He was willing to be eaten by the lion if God willed it so, but he never sought out a lion and made suggestions to it. He loved people too much to enjoy their enmity.

When he began to hold his great conventions criticism rose like a cloud of locusts and hovered over every city where he appeared. Editorial condemnation in current religious papers was scorching hot. Sarcasm, invective, solemn stupid arguments buttressed by carefully misused texts of Scripture, all were employed in an effort to discredit him in the eyes of the public. Of course the effort succeeded to some extent. For the rest of his days he bore the stigmata of what he called "questionable if not false, teaching." By many he was rejected outright. They had heard about those crackpot divine healing people and they would have none of it. They are not to be blamed for this. They were rejecting A. B. Simpson for the abuses practiced by others. They could not discriminate. All believers in the doctrine were by them tarred with the same stick. In spite of the obvious sincerity of the man himself, in spite of the thousands won to Christ through his labors, in spite of the Christ-centered, well-balanced message which he preached, and the dignity and decorum manifested in all his public meetings, he still had to endure misunderstanding and suspicion to the end of his days. And the Society he formed has, to some degree, inherited his cross.

CHAPTER TWELVE

By the cloud and the fire

Upon his recovery Mr. Simpson returned immediately to his duties as pastor of the Thirteenth Street Presbyterian Church. He felt like a man under sentence of death who had received a full pardon. Hope returned like a sunrise and his plans soared out again to meet the challenge of the unevangelized millions.

The old urge to reach the masses came back upon him with overwhelming force. Nearly two years before this he had accepted the call to the pastorate of the Thirteenth Street Church "with the explicit understanding on the part of the new church officers that they would unite with him in a popular religious movement to reach the unchurched masses." These are his own words. The church had never made good on that promise. They simply could not see it as he did. They had received a new impulse of life from the ministry of the new pastor. Attendance had stepped up and many members had been added to the rolls of the church, but the two viewpoints were irreconcilable. "They wanted a conventional parish

84

for respectable Christians. What their pastor wanted was a multitude of publicans and sinners." So Mr. Simpson explained later. If he could not inspire them to follow him, neither would he be hindered by them. He must follow his star. So he determined to resign his pastorate and launch out on his own. This step was taken only after a full week spent in earnest prayer. He would not trust to his own wisdom.

"The parting was most friendly," he assures us. "It is pleasant to look back to a crisis of so much importance passed without any strain whatever."

While the personal relationship between him and his church always remained warm and kindly, there were two circumstances which led him to feel that he should not only resign from the pastorate of his church but should retire from the Presbyterian ministry altogether. One was his experience of divine healing a few months before. His ministerial brethren were not unkind in their attitude toward him, but he knew his presence might easily prove embarrassing to them. The other was his being led to accept the doctrine of baptism by immersion as a scriptural teaching. He had been immersed himself after his miraculous recovery. Then he found that he could no longer in good conscience sprinkle helpless infants as required by the rules of the Presbyterian Church.

It is amusing to note that during his seminary days he had written a prize-winning paper in defense of infant baptism. Now he is withdrawing from his church because he no longer believes in the validity of his old thesis. "A foolish consistency," wrote Emerson, "is the hobgoblin of little minds, adored by little statesmen and philosophers and divines." A. B. Simpson was never a slave to consistency. He could sometimes contradict himself with an elegant grace that made the hide-bound "theologicians" wring their hands in impotent despair. For instance, he believed in immersion, was himself immersed, would administer baptism after no other mode. Yet he would receive into full membership in his church any child of God regardless of his stand on water baptism. He might pause before immersing a candidate long enough to ask a non-immersionist brother to lead in prayer! It was all very puzzling to the ecclesiastical stickler. But Mr. Simpson never saw anything incongruous about it. Neither was he always consistent in his application of the doctrine of divine healing to the requirements of actual life. The pitiful little syllogisms upon which some of his professed followers sometimes stretch poor distressed believers as upon a rack would have been summarily rejected by him. Kindness and love dictated his attitude toward the sick. He was more concerned with the leading of the Spirit and the prayer of faith than with rigid conformity to a doctrine—even his own doctrine.

His decision to quit his church and strike out alone into the work of evangelizing the multitudes of New York City looked to everyone except A. B. Simpson like a piece of rare folly. He had been earning five thousand dollars a year at his old job. Now he has exactly no income at all, and a family of seven to support. It looked like lunacy, and of course there was no lack of comforters to assure him that it was indeed lunacy. There were clergymen in the city who frankly stated their opinion that the brilliant young minister had lost his reason.

To trust God for his health was bad enough, but to trust for his daily bread as well—that was sure proof of insanity! The elders of his church came down to the parsonage the morning after the news broke, and offered their condolences to Mrs. Simpson. They felt, they said, "as if they had come to his funeral." "And it is possible," said Mr. Simpson afterwards, with dry humor, "that she may also have felt that he might as well be dead."

The wife of a prophet has no easy road to travel. She cannot always see her husband's vision, yet as his wife she must go along with him wherever his vision takes him. She is compelled therefore to walk by faith a good part of the time—and her husband's faith at that. Mrs. Simpson tried hard to understand but if she sometimes lost patience with her devoted but impractical husband she is not for that cause to be too much censured. From affluence and high social position she is called suddenly to poverty and near-ostracism. She must feed her large family somehow—and not one cent coming in. The salary has stopped, and the parsonage must be vacated! She tries to keep calm, but she is secretly frantic. And her husband's placid, "Now Margaret darling, don't get upset. God will provide," did not help too much. Mr. Simpson had heard the Voice ordering him out, and he went without fear. His wife had heard nothing, but she was compelled to go anyway. That she was a bit unsympathetic at times has been held against her by many. That she managed to keep within far sight of her absent-minded high soaring husband should be set down to her everlasting honor. It is no easy job being wife to such a man as A. B. Simpson was.

Mr. Simpson lost no time in getting started upon his new project. Through the newspapers (which for some reason were always interested in him) he announced a Sunday afternoon meeting to be held in a cheap place on Eighth Avenue known as Caledonian Hall where he would deliver an address on the spiritual needs of the city. He had specifically instructed his former parishioners not to attend the meetings. He did not wish to disturb the unity of Thirteenth Street Church. Only two persons disregarded his wishes and came. There was a fair crowd in attendance at that first meeting, though it must be acknowledged that New York managed to stay away in considerable numbers. That afternoon he announced his intention to launch a continuous campaign for the evangelization of the masses of the city, and invited all who were interested to meet him later for prayer and consultation. Only seven persons responded. But they were not discouraged. They knelt down and actually thanked God that they were poor and few and weak! And then they "threw themselves upon the might of the Holy Ghost." That was the rather inglorious beginning of what was to be one of the strongest forces for world-evangelization since the days of the apostles.

Sunday services continued at Caledonian Hall, with mid-week meetings at the Simpson home. Numbers increased greatly as the weeks went by, and scores were brought into the fold. A little organization was formed with the simplest kind of skeleton constitution. The new movement was on its way. The pastor had a little flock and the flock had his own spirit. They were all out for evangelism. Everyone went to work and sinners came flocking in. The crowds soon outgrew the hall, and the meetings had to be moved to larger quarters.

For the next eight years, or until the completion of their permanent home on Eighth Avenue, this band of peculiar people continued to move from place to place like the children of Israel in the wilderness. They were attempting a work so radically different that they had no precedent to guide them. They were compelled to learn by the hard and expensive method of trial and error. There were mistakes made and losses suffered as a result of bad business judgment or some unforeseen shift in human population or change in real estate values in a given locality. But the victories outweighed the defeats, and so they marched on. From hall to tent, from tent to theatre or on to some abandoned church went this happy band of soul-winners. Always they were busy at the one task to which they believed God had called them—that of bringing lost men to the Saviour, and always they were learning, were getting experience, were winning souls and adding to their number.

A. B. Simpson was in his glory. He was seeing Christian democracy at its simple best. No social lines separated his people from each other. His members came from every level of human society from the gutter to the penthouse. Any Saturday night " a brother of low degree" might be seen standing on a street corner giving his testimony while a well-to-do and cultured believer stood beside him holding his hat while he talked. It was a free church in the fullest sense of the word. The old irritating conservatism that used to block so many of his plans was gone. Gone were the paralyzing traditions that had

stopped his best efforts for so many years. No blessed
antiques were there, sitting solemnly about the church
building to woo the minds of the worshipers back into
the musty past. With the past they had little to do. Most
of them were glad to be rid of it. The future allured them
and the present kept them busy. There were no pew rents
and no assessments. The stranger and the poor were received with open arms. Their eloquent and scholarly pastor was their undisputed leader by common consent and
joyful acclaim. The meetings were marked by deep spir-
ituality and mighty flowing power. Altogether they presented as strange and as wonderful a sight as might have
been seen anywhere in Christendom as they preached
and sang and prayed their way through the wilderness
that was New York.

As the years went on Mr. Simpson and his people
came to see the need for a permanent base of operation,
located near the center of the city and built to meet the
needs of their work. They had become weary of the
hand-me-down buildings they had been forced to put up
with for so long. These were never satisfactory. A suitable location was accordingly chosen at the corner of
Eighth Avenue and West 44th Street, only one block
from Times Square, and plans were drawn up for the
new building. It was to provide a large auditorium for
the public meetings, three chapels for smaller gatherings,
an educational building for the Training Institute which
was already established, a book store on the ground floor
and a Missionary Home, or Christian hotel, with accom-
modations for about one hundred guests. The corner-

stone was laid in the fall of 1888 and the completed building dedicated in May 1889.

There was great rejoicing as the congregation moved into their new working quarters and set about the business to which they had given their lives. The Gospel Tabernacle, as the place was called (too bad they could not have thought of a *name* for it. But that was one rather unfortunate blind spot in the luminous mind of Simpson; he was never happy at choosing names), was the new home base, but it never became an end in itself. From there the busy workers radiated out like spokes from the hub of a wheel.

When the new work began under Mr. Simpson eight years before, there had been no thought of forming another church. They planned rather to carry on an aggressive evangelistic effort, leaving the converts free to join the churches of their own choice. But as the congregation grew, the clamor became insistent for a church home for the new believers. "Some wanted to be baptized," said Mr. Simpson later, "all wanted the Lord's supper and none wanted to be sent away." That was the cause back of the organization of a little church of less than twenty members. "At first there were not men enough to go around and fill the various offices, so some of our trustees had to be 'elect ladies.'" That was about seven years before the opening of the Gospel Tabernacle. By this time they had increased to a multitude which swarmed about the new center like swallows around an old chimney at sundown. The fame of the pastor and the wonder of his unique work had spread far abroad. From that time on they never suffered for lack of men.

CHAPTER THIRTEEN

Branches over the wall

There seems to be no satisfactory explanation for the astonishing activities of the Gospel Tabernacle over the next twenty years. At least there is no explanation on natural grounds. A veritable flood of spiritual energy appears to have been released through the consecration and faith of one man, Albert B. Simpson. It was as if a burning core of power had been tossed into the center of New York, radiating heat and light in all directions. Evangelistic and missionary zeal leaped out like fire. There was no want of workers. Everyone was expected to help, and almost everyone did. The work accomplished was almost beyond believing.

Several evenings during the week bands of young people from the Tabernacle held meetings on the streets. A number of rescue missions were opened and hundreds of human derelicts fished out and salvaged from the flotsam and jetsam of the lower classes. Groups of trained gospel workers visited the hospitals and jails every week with the message of hope. Earnest efforts were made to reach and rescue the fallen women that swarmed in certain sections of the city. A free dispensary was maintained for the poor of that neighborhood known grimly as "Hell's Kitchen." Special services were held for the sailors that crowded the water fronts. An orphanage was opened for the poor of the city streets, and other efforts made to relieve the destitute and the suffering wherever they were found within the great melting pot that is New York.

Several organizations were formed from the teeming life·of the Tabernacle fellowship, each with a specific object in view and with a particular function to perform. For instance there were no less than six young people's societies, all going full blast at one and the same time! There was no overlapping. They knew what they were called to do, and they did it with enthusiasm.

These many outside activities were the overflow from the great public services held at the Tabernacle every Sunday. At these services Mr. Simpson himself usually preached, though many other celebrated preachers appeared in his pulpit from time to time. A large Sunday School was maintained, and to supplement its work a class in the catechism was held each week for all children who desired to attend. An early morning service was held each Sunday in German. Rev. A. E. Funk, an assistant pastor, who spoke the German language fluently, was in charge of this service.

Curiously enough, there was also an Episcopal service of Holy Communion conducted each Sunday at the Tabernacle. Dr. Henry Wilson, an Episcopal clergyman, officiated. He never left the fold of the Episcopal Church, but obtained permission from his bishop to erect an altar in one of the chapels of the Tabernacle for this service. He was a saintly character and a warm friend of Mr. Simpson to the end of his days.

Of a piece with these local activities, but of greater importance than all of them, was the foreign missions enterprise which sprang out of the zealous heart of A. B. Simpson.

He had come to New York with the express purpose of putting himself in a position to more effectively prosecute the work of world evangelization. While still connected with the Thirteenth Street Church he had launched a missionary journal, *The Gospel in All Lands*—the first illustrated missionary magazine to be published on the North American continent. He was forced by his physical collapse to relinquish the editorship of this magazine, but under other management it continued for many years, the model and inspiration for all similar publications which sprang into print later.

Soon after the opening of his independent work he began to publish another missionary monthly called by the uneuphonious name, *The Word, Work and World*. In spite of its name it was undoubtedly one of the finest missionary journals ever published by any religious society anywhere. The sweep and range of it are amazing. Its editor had taken the world for his parish. In its pages his mighty earth-covering wing-stretch became apparent, probably for the first time.

It was partly through this magazine that A. B. Simpson began to attract wide notice as a missionary leader. He kept it world-wide in its scope and interdenominational in its interests. The affairs of the leading missionary societies of the world were reported with warm sympathy and interesting detail. News of the doings of the great evangelists and other popular religious leaders appeared regularly. Every important gathering of spiritual leaders in all parts of the world received friendly notice and intelligent comment. Illuminating articles on almost every phase of life in missionary lands, well written, scholarly, yet warmly evangelical, were regular features. And to focus attention each issue of the magazine contained a generous number of carefully done illustrations printed by means of the then-popular wood cut. In spite of the advances made in the art of journalism since that time, the old brown copies of *The Word, Work and World* which we possess today still remain excellent examples of *how* to edit a missionary magazine.

Interest in the work of foreign missions was growing both in Europe and in North America. The dramatic success of great men such as Livingstone and others had fired the imagination of the public. Encouraged by the labors of others, but urged forward by his own impelling vision of the lost world with its millions "in mute anguish, wringing their hands," Mr. Simpson determined to do something definite about the whole thing—not simply to favor it, to write about it—but to engage in it, to make it the work of his life. Indeed he must do this. The inward pressure was destroying him. There was no escape. A missionary society was being born out of a heart big with love for God and the perishing world.

They tell deep stories of those days, stories distilled from the restrained public utterances of the man himself, or whispered reverently by some close friend who was permitted to look into his heart for a brief moment it may be, stories of tears and long prayer vigils, of lonely walks by the sea shore in the dead of night when others were in their beds asleep, when the moan of the sea sounded like the cry of lost souls, and every grain of sand along the shore appeared to be a dying man. These stories concern the real history of A. B. Simpson and the work that grew out of his strong passion. The colorful deeds of his public ministry were possible only because of these little-publicized experiences of his inward life where the Christ of Gethsemane came near to travail again through a man utterly yielded.

As far back as 1883, while still in the old Twenty-third Street Tabernacle, Mr. Simpson had inaugurated a new type of meeting, which he called a missionary convention. This was original only in the sense that it achieved for the first time a synthesis of the best features of several other kinds of public meeting, and succeeded in producing in one place and at once a Bible conference, a camp meeting, an evangelistic campaign and a missionary promotional meeting. So highly successful were these conventions that they soon spread to many cities of the United States and Canada and drew to their platform some of the world's leading preachers and missionary leaders. By 1887 they had become famous. Thousands flocked to them in the great cities of the North American continent. One strong attraction was the teaching of divine healing and the practice of praying for the sick. Another was the presence of returned missionaries. Real live missionaries were sufficiently rare in those days to guarantee a crowd wherever they appeared.

At first Mr. Simpson was able personally to direct these conventions. He carried a heavy preaching schedule at most of them for the first few years, but he was too humble and too shrewd a leader to permit the success of these gatherings to depend too much upon his own ministry. So he invited workers from everywhere. The great, the famous, the gifted from all over the world (and some who were neither famous nor great, but who were his personal friends whom he delighted to honor) would be concentrated in one city and on one platform for a great series of meetings lasting anywhere from two to ten days. The number of workers assembled by the big-hearted Simpson often inspired caustic comment or good-natured ribbing from the public. "You know, brother," said Mr. Simpson once when discussing this with a friend, "they say the number of speakers on my convention platforms makes my announcements look like a small-town telephone directory. But I have a good reason for all that. I want to enjoy the broadest fellowship possible myself, and I want my people to receive the benefit of the ministry of all God's gifted servants, regardless of whether they agree with me in everything or not."

As these conventions grew in importance they quite naturally drew the fire of that large section of the Christian public which was opposed to all the doctrines and practices for which Mr. Simpson stood. And it must be admitted that they who were against him were far greater in number (and usually in influence) than they who were for him. His old friends, the newspapers, began

7

to poke fun at his great conventions. Now and again an artist, seeking a popular subject for a cartoon to fill his daily schedule, would hit upon Simpson and his "Faith Cure Convention," and the result would be a picture, making merry at his expense. The religious journals of the country were divided over him. Some of them published scorching denunciations; others defended him vigorously. There were two points of attack. One was his teaching on divine healing, the other his missionary zeal. Some of the leaders could not forgive him for his ability to raise more missionary money in ten days than they could do in ten years.

The famous Presbyterian clergyman, Dr. A. T. Pierson, once wrote an article in a religious magazine criticizing Simpson and his method of raising missionary funds. A noticeable decline in missionary receipts followed from the time the article appeared in print. A few months later Dr. Pierson had a change of heart and wrote another article retracting his first statements and giving Simpson a clean bill of health. Immediately the missionary income zoomed back to normal! A beautiful example of the Christ-like spirit of the man Pierson and fine proof of the tremendous influence which he exerted over the Christian public.

The unfriendly attitude of the rank and file of church members toward what came to be known as the "Full Gospel" or the "deeper life"—by which is meant the baptism of the Spirit and divine healing—set A. B. Simpson to dreaming again. His dream concerned an *alliance* of like-minded Christians the world over who were hungry for a better and more satisfying life in Christ. It was not to be a split off of an existing body, not an organized protest, neither a society to provide protection from some outside enemy. Rather it was to be a fellowship, a communion of saints, a simple bond uniting believers everywhere whose hearts were hungry for the deeper things of God.

In 1885 Mr. Simpson attended a conference on the deeper life in Bethshan, London. From that conference he came away convinced that the time had come to put his dream into action. Two years later, after the necessary preliminary work had been done, at the summer convention at Old Orchard, Maine, the Christian Alliance was formally organized. The simplest form of constitution was drawn up to give direction to the new society.

The same convention that saw the birth of the Christian Alliance saw also the beginning of another society, the Evangelical Missionary Alliance. This society was called into being to provide a more efficient means of carrying on the work of foreign missions to which Mr. Simpson and his people were dedicated. The lack of any unified strategy for the prosecution of the task was proving to be a source of embarrassment. A new missionary zeal was spreading throughout the entire country, and it must have intelligent direction. There was too much lost motion, too much that was merely hit and miss. Something had to be done, and the time seemed to be ripe. Something was done. Before the Convention had broken up that year at Old Orchard the Evangelical Missionary Alliance had been launched.

It was as simple as the Christian Alliance. Its principles were brief but clear. It was an undenominational society for the rapid evangelization of the most neglected sections of the foreign mission field, using laymen and laywomen as well as regular ministers to carry on its work. It pledged itself to rigid economy, guaranteed no salaries, and required of its workers a life of simple faith. It would be directed by a central board which would be elected annually. Two years later the name was changed to the International Missionary Alliance. Mr. Simpson was elected General Secretary.

The two societies continued to operate separately for a matter of ten years, though the business meetings of the two boards might be held in the same room on the same evening one after the other with scarcely a member rising to leave upon the adjournment of the first meeting. The personnel would hardly be changed. The secretary would simply open a different book! The Christion Alliance supported the International Missionary Alliance though it could have no voice in its affairs. As a member of one society Mr. Smith might decide to undertake some missionary project, and then he would have to wait till the board of the other society met—of which he was also a member—before he could be sure that he would have his own consent to finance the project! It was very confusing, but with the charming inconsistency which often marked both societies this condition was tolerated till the year 1897. Then they got around to the taking of an important step toward better management. That year the two societies were formally joined in wedlock. The twain become one flesh and have not been sundered since that time.

Apparently neither society wanted to give up its

name, so they struck a compromise and kept both of them, which, with minor omissions, they solemnly hung on the new one. The result is a wonderful society with a name too long and awkward to handle without a pinch bar, The Christian and Missionary Alliance. Asked what society they represent its members may be seen to brace themselves, take a deep breath, and begin to recite. And worse than all, nobody ever understands it the first time. Along about the fourth time through the inquirer will take courage, smile, and begin timidly to repeat it experimentally, a world of unbelief in his face. It requires no prophetic gift to see that The Christian and Missionary Alliance represents a magnificent triumph of holy zeal over bad nomenclature.

Mr. Simpson however considered the name a happy one. "It expresses the genius of our movement." said he. "We are an alliance of Christians for world wide missionary work." That would seem to settle it. But we still wish the idea could be expressed without such a tax on the memory and with less wear on the vocal cords.

CHAPTER FOURTEEN

He goes out and comes in

The Christian and Missionary Alliance looms so large in the life of A. B. Simpson that we dare not pass it over with a few paragraphs if we are to get even a fair picture of the man himself. It was a movement first—an organization second, an organization at all only because some kind of track was necessary to determine which direction the movement should take. It was loosely constructed, with "just enough executive machinery to hold it together and make it effective." But it had movement first, motion. Indeed these had to be wherever Simpson was. He never knew the meaning of static Christianity.

His society is himself grown large. It is the child of his heart, and it resembles its father as all good children should. The same humility is seen in it to this day, the same distrust of the flesh, the same preoccupation with the person of Christ. And his faults appear in it too, his impatience with details, his lack of organizational ability, his unwillingness to face things squarely and fight them through. He would always rather pray and trust that everything would come out all right—and usually it did.

For thirty years he continued to lead the society which he had formed, and never for the least division of a moment did he forget or permit the society to forget the purpose for which it was brought into being. Always, everywhere, through his writings and his public utterances he kept driving home its objectives. "It is to hold up Jesus in His fullness, 'the same yesterday, and today, and forever!' It is to lead God's hungry children to know their full inheritance of privilege and blessing for spirit, soul and body. It is to encourage and incite the people of God to do the neglected work of our age and time among the unchurched classes at home and the perishing heathen abroad."

He never intended his society to become a denomination. Whether this proves superior insight or the total lack of it, history will decide. He sought to provide a fellowship only, and looked with suspicion upon anything like rigid organization. He wanted the Alliance to be a spiritual association of believers who hungered to know the fullness of the blessing of the Gospel of Christ, working concertedly for the speedy evangelization of the world.

Thus conceived the whole thing was simple. But the law of growth is always from the simple to the complex. The society had not been long in existence before normal developments within it began to upset the idyllic simplicity of the original plan. "There were cases constantly arising," admitted Mr. Simpson, "where it was necessary to provide special and permanent religious privileges for little bands of Christians who had either been converted in some evangelistic meeting or pushed out of their churches by false teaching and harsh pressure and prejudice." Necessity forced the society to care for these orphans. They would not be put off with idealistic sentiments. They wanted a church home in which to bring up their families. They wanted to be baptized, to enjoy the privilege of the Lord's Supper, to have a place where they could be married, and from which they might be buried when their summons came. The society had to meet these demands or go out of business.

This put Mr. Simpson and his people in a tough spot. After much consultation they at last saw light. They would not leave their first love. They would continue as they had begun, no denomination, but a spiritual fellowship merely. However, in order that the various orphan flocks throughout the country might enjoy the Christian privileges which were rightfully theirs, gifted men should be appointed to care for them, and they would call them not pastors, but Local Superintendents. So it was done. These groups were placed under the care of qualified shepherds—not pastors, be it remembered—they merely assumed all the duties, enjoyed all the privileges and performed all the labors of pastors! They were Local Superintendents!

After half a century the society remains substantially as it was first created—a growing, aggressive, dynamic movement for world evangelization, the only such body on the face of the earth that does not know what it is. It gently but persistently declares that it is not a denomination, and yet it exercises every spiritual and ecclesiastical function of any Protestant body in the world —without one exception. Sweet ignorance that can be entrusted with individual responsibility for the evangelization of 79 million heathen souls, that can command over one million dollars a year in cold cash toward the work of foreign missions, that can continue each year to preach the Gospel in over one hundred languages on twenty pioneer fields of the world, that turns out from its Bible schools an ever increasing stream of trained and gifted missionary candidates for work in the regions beyond! Maybe there is a Biblical explanation for all this: "For whether we be beside ourselves, it is to God: or whether we be sober, it is for your cause. For the love of Christ constraineth us."

Mr. Simpson was a premillenarian, but the doctrine would not lie quiet in his heart. Like the other tenets of his creed it would take hands and feet and go to work at the one mighty job of winning men to God. He held that the return of Christ depended upon a world-wide proclamation of the Gospel. This belief was not merely incidental. It became one of the great motivating forces in his missionary endeavors. He preached it constantly and even set it to music and sang it:

> *The Master's coming draweth near,*
> *The Son of Man will soon appear,*
> *His kingdom is at hand.*
> *But ere that glorious day can be,*
> *This gospel of the kingdom, we*
> *Must preach in every land.*

The teaching expressed in the closing lines of this stanza is open to question. Careful exegetes will probably deny its correctness, and some may, as a consequence, reject the whole missionary program with which it is associated. But cutting through the pro and con arguments and stripping away all fancy exegesis we come to two simple truths: First, Jesus Christ is absent from the earth, and will return again in glory when His present work is accomplished. Second, it is the imperative obligation of the Church to preach the Gospel to every creature, and to keep on preaching it till He does return. That is what it means to his society today, and that is all it ever meant in practice to Mr. Simpson himself. And almost every premillenarian will agree with this position.

While the work of foreign missions was always Mr. Simpson's first love, it did not by any means absorb all the amazing energies of the man. There was his Tabernacle, a great central factory, sending out its conveyor belts in all directions. For all its activities he was almost wholly responsible. Then, he usually had a new project brewing, a school or an orphanage or another mission. Some of his plans succeeded, other failed, but win or lose he was sure to be back the next week with another plan, patiently talking his board into sponsoring it. Or, if they could not see it, he would be likely to launch out alone, trusting God to help him through with it.

The need for special training for missionaries and home workers early led to the establishing of a Bible and missionary training school. Under various names and in different locations this school operated from 1883 on, ultimately settling down at Nyack, New York, in a beautiful spot along the Hudson River, twenty-five miles above New York City. There for forty-six years it has continued to flourish, turning out every year a large class of trained workers for service at home as well as on the foreign field.

Another project arose directly out of Mr. Simpson's teaching on healing for the physical body. He felt the need of some quiet place where sick and discouraged persons might find a sympathetic atmosphere and opportunity to wait on God for deliverance from their bodily ails. The burden became so great that he finally turned his own home over for this purpose. This was done over the protests of his wife. There were children in the Simpson household, and she argued that they should be raised in a home, not in an institution. She was undoubtedly right in her position. The difficulties Mr. Simpson later experienced in bringing his children to Christ may be attributed in part to the fact that they had been sacrificed altogether too far in the interest of their father's public ministry. We have every right to sacrifice ourselves, but that we have any right to sacrifice our children without their consent may, with reason, be vigorously denied. That he encountered bitter opposition from his family at times must be admitted if we are to tell the whole truth. The idea that he may have brought some of this upon himself by unwise acts cannot be wholly ruled out. He may have sometimes forgotten that God had called him to be a husband and a father as well as a minister of the Gospel.

This Home for Prayer and Physical Healing, as it was called, after it had been moved to several different locations and its name had been changed to Berachah, was finally settled at Nyack. There it proved to be a rare blessing to hundreds of suffering persons for many years to come.

We dare not pass over one project which, fortunately, we believe, turned out to be a failure. Mr. Simpson at one time fathered a plan to create near Nyack an Alliance center where persons in sympathy with the doctrines and practices of The Christian and Missionary Alliance might buy property, build homes, and live sequestered from the contaminating influences of the world. A company was formed consisting of A. B. Simpson, A. E. Funk, and David Crear. A large square of real estate was purchased, lots were laid out and offered for sale to the members of the society. Everything looked rosy except for one minor difficulty—nobody would buy! Alliance people simply were not interested. After trying vainly to make the plan work they at last abandoned it altogether. The conscientious Mr. Simpson, scrupulously honest and self-sacrificing, as he always was, shouldered the blame, bought out his partners, and took the loss himself.

The failure of this project was a great kindness from God to his servant. Love and zeal had inspired the idea, but it had been a mistake, nevertheless. An honest mistake it had been, but a big one. When Simpson succeeded it was in a big way. When he failed he made great failures. It had to be so. Men of his caliber do not make little mistakes. They fly too high and too far to steer their courses by city maps. They ask not, "What street is that?" but "What continent?" And when they get off of the course for a moment they will be sure to pull up a long way from their goal. Their range and speed make this inevitable. Little men who never get outside of their own yards point to these mistakes with great satisfaction. But history has a way of disposing of these critics by filing them away in quiet anonymity. She cannot be bothered to preserve their names. She is too busy chalking up the great successes and huge failures of her favorites.

All the while that he was launching his various projects—and watching them sink in the harbor or sweep out triumphantly on the bosom of the deep—he was promoting by means of his conventions a highly successful continuous campaign of missionary evangelism throughout the United States and Canada. At the same time he was directing a growing army of missionaries on an ever increasing number of foreign mission fields. The work was booming. No one could question that. Fortunately the society preserved its flexibility under the strain of growth, and by means of some nice footwork it managed to cope with every emergency that arose with the years and the expanding work.

Add to all this the editing of a top-flight missionary magazine (which shuttled through a series of changes and became at last *The Alliance Weekly*, as which it still flourishes), the managing of a publishing concern, and the writing of innumerable songs, books and magazine articles, and you get some idea of how much work A. B. Simpson managed to turn out. And this, the emaciated, "cadaverous-looking" minister upon whom science had tacked the death sentence a few years before! It is so, verily, explain it as we may. Mr. Simpson never doubted what the explanation was. "It is the Lord," he had said after that pine forest experience, and the passing of the years never brought him reason to change his mind about it.

CHAPTER FIFTEEN

He dances before the ark

For thirty years Mr. Simpson served the church which his devotion had called into being. It was during the long years of his pastorate there that his greatest work was accomplished. The buildings next to the Tabernacle were called "Headquarters," but the true headquarters for The Christian and Missionary Alliance was the pulpit of the Gospel Tabernacle, where for more than a quarter of a century the missionary pastor continued to pour forth his mighty sermons.

In the history of world evangelization Simpson's Gospel Tabernacle must be accorded a position out of all proportion to its size or physical appearance. For sheer spiritual output and for far-reaching influence upon the whole evangelical religious world it has probably never had an equal in the United States. The building itself was the architectural embodiment of that verse which was the life text of its founder, "Not by might, nor by power, but by my Spirit, saith the Lord of Hosts."

Whoever first named the Tabernacle the "Cave of

111

Adullam" had not only a fine sense of humor, but a nice eye for similarities as well. Taking into account the building and all the circumstances that gave it birth, no more accurate descriptive tag could have been found for the place. The founder—so much like David in so many ways—had literally escaped from the cold unfriendly religion of his time and had here gathered to himself a company of adventurous persons who became his devoted followers and ardent backers of the work he was called to do. Many who at first resorted to him were "in distress, and discontented," and they found in the Tabernacle fellowship a sweet refuge from the past. Later the work came to be made up very largely of those who had been converted through the efforts of the Tabernacle itself, but its first beginnings ran a close parallel with the story of David and the cave of Adullam.

The building itself is so ordinary looking as to surprise and disappoint one who sees it for the first time. It takes not too much imagination to picture this as a cave in a wilderness, and to hear the sound of a harp floating out from its somewhat dingy interior. Crushing in upon the Tabernacle building, shutting out almost every ray of God's good sunshine, are the Headquarters offices and the Alliance Home. These are housed in a building six stories high which is served by a pocket-sized elevator with a mean cruising speed of one or two floors occasionally. As far back as the year 1907 Mr. Simpson is on record as stating that he felt that they had outgrown their facilities and suggesting that another and more suitable building be erected. For some reason nothing came of this. The buildings remain today, except for minor changes, about as they were originally built.

It was never the building that interested the people. They accepted it as a work shop in which the fine work of the Lord might be done, and out from which skilled artificers might go to repeat the work in all corners of the earth. To this gospel center for a generation came the leading preachers of all denominations. Popular evangelists, leading Christian educators, pioneer missionaries, famed pulpit orators from every part of the world gravitated to this humble place either to preach in its famous pulpit or to slip in quietly and listen that they might know for themselves whether those things were indeed true which they had heard away there in London, or Hong Kong, or Buenos Aires.

The pulpit of the Gospel Tabernacle was open to any honest man who had a call from God to preach the Gospel. The leading preachers of the world were heard there from time to time, but so real was the humility of its pastor that he would often sit quietly by and hear with appreciation men of very modest gifts indeed. If they could win souls that was recommendation enough. "But they are the Lord's children," he would say when some friend chided him for inviting certain men into his pulpit. It never seemed to bother him that a speaker was of inferior platform ability, and he appeared wholly innocent of the glaring contrast between himself and his guest. No matter who entered his pulpit, he overshadowed them without effort. He was not the most popular, but he was one of the most gifted pulpit masters of his generation.

113

"He was a minstrel," said Dr. Leon Tucker, "a spiritual minstrel; preaching was melodious and musical when it fell from his lips." "Ah, but you should have heard Jenny Lind," some of the old-timers were wont to say when someone praised another singer in their hearing. They felt that they had heard the sum of all song incarnate when they had listened to the incredibly beautiful voice of the "Swedish Nightingale." The preaching of A. B. Simpson often had some such effect upon those who heard it.

One coming into the Gospel Tabernacle or into any of the Convention halls where he appeared up and down the country in the days of his greatness might have experienced quite literally something like the following: The "preliminaries" are finished and it is time for the sermon. Mr. Simpson steps forward, pauses for a moment, and then in a low reverent tone announces his text. The tense silence is broken only by the voice of the speaker. His early training has given him a quiet reserve. He never acquired, or quickly rid himself of the stilted manners and holy tones common to the pulpit. His manner is relaxed and natural as he faces his hearers. Large framed, impressive and dignified, his very appearance gives promise of a great message to follow. He begins to speak with the Bible out-spread on one hand and the other hand resting lightly upon his hip. At first the words come slowly, spoken in a rich baritone of remarkable range and power. As he warms to his theme the speed of utterance increases, his voice takes on mounting degrees of emotional intensity while his body sways back and forth rhythmically, a kind of human metronome keeping

114

time to the music of his words. His gestures are few, but when moved more than usual he lays his Bible down, places both hands on his hips and shakes his great head to emphasize a point. The effect of these gestures is tremendous. The lofty truth he is proclaiming, the strong, magnetic quality of his voice, the swift flow of his language, all combine to produce an impression so profound that when he is through speaking and the benediction is pronounced the listeners sit in hushed silence, unable or unwilling to break the spell of the sermon.

The sermons themselves were models of structural perfection, and his diction such that a stenographic report of his messages might be published with little or no editing. This was a result partly of his ability to "think on his feet," and partly of his early habit of writing out his sermons in full before delivering them.

As to what type of preacher he was, he seems to have been a blend of many types. There are those who insist that he was primarily an expository preacher. Some say he used the topical method, and others insist that he was a textual preacher pure and simple. The truth seems to be that he was sufficiently versatile to use any method the occasion might require. His printed sermons show a flair for symbolism in their theology. No man could compare with him in making the Bible illustrate itself. He could make theology sing as few men have been able to do. He never uttered a cold fact of doctrine. In his mouth doctrine became warm and living. He was preeminently a Christ preacher. He believed the Bible existed to show forth Jesus, and the face of the Lord of Glory might be seen peering out from almost any sentence or paragraph of the Old Testament or the New when Simpson was doing the preaching. Greater expositors than Simpson there have been, but few have equaled him in his ability to reach the human heart. His utter love for the person of Jesus was responsible for this.

After his experience of the anointing of the Holy Spirit he was for the rest of his days an enraptured Christian. His enjoyment of the presence of the indwelling Christ almost literally transported him. His was a ravished heart which seemed to know no limit in its ardent devotion to the person of the Saviour. It was inevitable that a heart so ecstatic should sing, that the thoughts proceeding from a mind so enchanted should dance before the ark of God.

There seemed to be at the time Simpson began his work no hymnody expressing his particular type of mysticism. Wesley was happy in having ready at hand a poet who could catch his spirit and set his movement to music. Simpson had no such poet. No lyric medium existed for the expression of his spiritual raptures. He must create one for himself. So he wrote songs, and sang them, and did very well everything considered.

His first songs were written not as songs, but as poetic conclusions to his sermons. He liked to close a message gracefully with a stanza or two of verse, summing up in a few lines the burden of his message. Later he ventured to have these verses set to music and sung either as a solo or by the congregation at the close of the sermon. As he grew surer footed in this unaccustomed field he began to one-finger out the melody himself and call in his song leader, Mr. J. H. Burke, May Agnew or his

116

daughter Margaret to complete the harmonization. Another musician who composed the music for some of his songs and who did much to help create the hymnody which came to be a part of the Alliance, was Captain R. Kelso Carter. He was a naval man, an instructor at Annapolis, and an outspoken Christian. He was a man of strong but eccentric character whose songs, while marked by traces of superior gift, were nevertheless too militant and boisterous for the average Christian to enjoy.

The hymnal which has had the greatest influence within the Alliance movement is *Hymns of the Christian Life,* compiled about the year 1905 by Simpson, Burke, Stebbins and others. The book has its weaknesses, but for all that we are willing to go out on a limb and say that there was never another like it since the art of printing was invented. For glowing spiritual power, for warmth of devotion, for rapturous preoccupation with the loveliness of Jesus, for passionate outreaching toward the ends of the earth it has never had, and in my estimation is not likely to have, an equal under the sun. Here as nowhere else the almost incredible wingspread of the man Simpson is seen. In that book he literally brooded over the whole earth with love and tears and pity.

We promised at the beginning to "leave the warts in." Simple truth requires us to state that A. B. Simpson does not rate high as a writer of hymns. The effort on the part of some of his admirers to place him along with Watts and Wesley is simply absurd.

A hymn, to be great—to be a hymn at all—must meet certain simple requirements. 1. It must have literary excellence. 2. It must be compact enough to be sung easily. 3. It must express the religious feelings of the Universal Church. 4. The music must have dignity and reserve.

On none of these counts could Mr. Simpson's compositions qualify. His poetry lacked literary finish. The central idea might be poetic, but his craftsmanship was not equal to the task of expressing it. His singing heart sometimes betrayed him into attempting to sing things that simply were not lyrical and could not be sung. The virtue of brevity also was lacking in most of his songs. He sometimes rambled on into eight and ten verses, and if by happy chance he got through before the eighth verse he was sure to append a chorus that would run down over the next page. The minister in him overcame the poet, so that when he attempts to write a song the sermonic division is apparent at once. With few exceptions his songs are simply sermons in verse, the whole thing being there before us in plain sight, the introduction, the various "points" and the conclusion. But it is in the music that his songs suffer the most. A few of his compositions can be sung, but the most of them can be negotiated by none except trained singers. The transitions are too abrupt and the range too great for the ordinary congregation.

There can be no doubt about it, Mr. Simpson wrote too much poetry, or at least too much of it has been published. He could produce good strong, if ordinary, verse, and it is to be regretted that so much got into print which is not only very poor but is certainly far below what he was able to do at his best. In rushing into print with certain of his casual poems his friends have done him no small disfavor. Much is said there in bad verse which he could have said in beautiful prose at a great saving to his reputation as a writer.

"Scorn not the sonnet," wrote Wordsworth, "with this key Shakespeare unlocked his heart." "The less Shakespeare he," replied the forthright Browning. The less Simpson for some of his poetry. Only a big man could live down such a failure. And he has done it triumphantly.

After saying all this I would yet confess that hardly a day goes by that I do not kneel and sing, in a shaky baritone comfortably off key, the songs of Simpson. They feed my heart and express my longings, and I can find no other's songs that do this in as full a measure. Of his songs—there are 155 of them in the old *Hymns of the Christian Life* alone—only about three have attained to anything like wide popularity, and not above a dozen are heard even in the gatherings of The Christian and Missionary Alliance. Yet it is my sober judgment that Simpson has put into a few of his songs more of awful longing, of tender love, of radiant trust, of hope and worship and triumph than can be found in all the popular gospel songs of the last hundred years put together. Those songs are simply not to be compared with his. Simpson's songs savor of the holy of holies, the outstretched wings of the cherubim and the Shekinah glory. The others speak of the outer court and the milling crowd.

For all their technical flaws, the songs of Simpson— the few singable ones—became a powerful factor toward the success of The Christian and Missionary Alliance. They helped tremendously to impart that intangible something we call *flavor* to the meetings of the Society. There is a triumphant quality about some of them scarcely to be found in any other hymns. They have been used to inspire young men and women to wonderful acts of unselfish devotion. The wail of the lost world and the yearning sorrow of Jesus over the "other sheep" are heard in the missionary songs. No wonder the altars were always crowded with missionary volunteers. And how they sang! After all the years, the singing of "Alliance hymns" by a congregation of self-sacrificing ministers and work-weary missionaries at some conference or convention still comes as a revelation to my heart.

Simpson's songs were more than songs; they were slogans. Their value to the Society lay in their power to compress into a single sentence a cluster of dynamic ideas and to set those ideas singing in the hearts of believing men. Simpson—consciously or unconsciously, I am not sure which—was a master sloganeer, the greatest ever called to the service of the Church. He could take a Bible phrase, or a phrase adapted from the Bible, shape it into what he loved to call a "watchword," and set multitudes to singing it. In a few of these musical slogans you can read the doctrines and policy of The Christian and Missionary Alliance: "Jesus Only," "The Same Yesterday, To-day, and Forever," "Himself," "Christ in Me," "The Fullness of Jesus," "I Will Say Yes to Jesus," "I Take, He Undertakes," "Nothing Is Too Hard for Jesus," "Launch Out," "Go and Tell Them," "To the Regions Beyond," "Jesus Giveth Us the Victory," "I Am Living in the Glory," "Even as He." There in concentration you will find the genius of the man and his movement.

CHAPTER SIXTEEN

Down to earth

Rev. A. B. Simpson was a great preacher. "The greatest whose voice has been heard in New York City in twenty-five years," Dr. Marquis said of him when that voice had been stilled by death. But he was no business man. In the light of the plain facts, Thompson's remark, "Had business been his calling, some think he would have been one of the large financiers," deserves no more than a smile.

To succeed in business requires that a man have a sympathy with the earth, an affinity for, and keen understanding of, the rough and tumble life of the world. These Mr. Simpson assuredly had not. He could come down to earth sometimes when necessity was thrust upon him, but he belonged on the wing, and he trod the earth but awkwardly when he was forced down. Even the eagle must descend occasionally to secure her food, but the earth is not her element. She is at her best only when she has a thousand feet of clean air beneath her broad wings.

121

Simpson had not the tough, fibrous mind necessary to fight his way to success in the business world. He was too idealistic, too gentle. He was so trusting that he would not watch out for sharp practices in others, and it never occurred to him that anyone should doubt *him*. When reminded once that a note would fall due at a New York bank the next day he turned to an assistant and said casually, "Go tell them to hold it a week." He could not see the humor in such a remark. He would have been willing to "hold it a week" for others; why should they not do the same for him?

Though illy equipped to manage a paying business he early took a stand that made some kind of secular income necessary to him. He determined to imitate Paul who at one period in his life preached the Gospel "without charge" and worked for his own living. He refused to accept any salary, either from his Tabernacle or from the Society of which he was the head. So popular was he with a certain devoted stratum of the Christian public that he might easily have had anything he chose to command by way of monetary reward. His followers were generous almost beyond believing. (Even today The Christian and Missionary Alliance stands year after year at or near the top for per capita giving among all religious bodies.) He could with perfect justice have accepted a salary large enough to amply support his large family. He chose not to do this. Every cent that came into his coffers by way of contributions went to support the work of the Society.

Mr. Simpson's personal income was derived from various business enterprises which he conducted in New

York City. One of these was a restaurant, the actual management of which was in the hands of his son, Howard. This was a perpetual headache, and never netted him anything but grief. He also ran a book store which proved to be a fine outlet for promotional literature for foreign missions but which brought in almost nothing by way of profits. In addition to these he also maintained a commercial printing concern in the city. This business was a fair success in a small way, and managed to bring in enough income to enable him to support his family in modest comfort.

A. E. Thompson, in his *Life of A. B. Simpson,* says, "There can be no question that his business was the great burden that finally proved too heavy for him." This may be disputed, for Mr. Simpson lived to be seventy-six years of age—a good old age for anyone, business or no business. However, the statement is valuable in that it is the opinion of a close friend of Simpson's with whom he must often have discussed his personal affairs.

To finance one after another of his religious ventures he would sometimes borrow sums of money ranging anywhere from a few dollars to several thousand. For many years he managed to pray his way out of these financial holes, meeting every obligation fully; but in his declining years he found himself so deeply in debt that he was forced to turn to friends for assistance. All his undertakings had been entirely in the open. His own life had been free from any taint of covetousness or fraud. His debts represented the bad breaks which he had encountered in attempting to save the lost or minister relief to the suffering and the poor. He had meant only to do all he could to lift the weight of human suffering from the hearts of men. His judgment had not always been sound. Of his heart there was never any doubt.

Knowing the man and the circumstances a few of his well-to-do friends chipped in and paid him out in full. This enabled him to die solvent, but he left nothing of any value to his family.

His inability to provide for his family as sumptuously after he gave up his five-thousand-dollar salary, as he had been able to do before, did not make for peace in the Simpson home. Mrs. Simpson was not at first able to see her husband's vision. She could not sympathize with his radical stand on money matters. Her practical nature would not be content with anything as intangible as faith. On more than one occasion she found herself without a cent to meet the heavy demands of the household. At such times Mr. Simpson would commit the whole affair to God in prayer and then go blithely about his business. His wife would stay home, look after the children, and do the worrying. He was much criticized for refusing to accept the salary which was rightfully his, but he steadfastly refused to change his position. He felt that he knew what God expected of him and his peace lay in doing God's will as he understood it. Not until his old age did he receive one cent from his spiritual labors, and then only because the men of his board issued a good-natured ultimatum and compelled him to agree to receive a small allowance for his last days.

We do not want to create the impression that Mr. Simpson was a visionary, a man wholly impractical. When necessary he was capable of sharp judgment and

124

swift action. On one occasion a low character came into his office and attempted to extort money from him by blackmail. Secure in his conscious innocence he refused to enter into argument with the man. He simply lay hold of the back of his neck, marched him out into the hall, and tossed him downstairs! This seems so out of mood with the gentle character of the man of God that some may doubt the veracity of the story. But the incident is well attested. The force of gravitation may have aided somewhat the blackmailer's descent to the street, but that the original impulse to descend came from Mr. Simpson himself has been established beyond a reasonable doubt.

He was, from his childhood, possessed of unusual physical charm. His few photographs—he was shy of the camera most of his life—indicates that, while his appearance naturally changed with the years, he remained through every stage of his development a most strikingly handsome person. There is reason to believe that he was in his early years a rather natty dresser, something of a Beau Brummel, indeed, or the clerical equivalent of it. With the deepening of his spiritual life he lost interest in outward appearances, and though his presence was always impressive when on the platform, in his later years he showed some evidences of preoccupation. His oversize sack coat appeared to have been cut out originally for Goliath, his vest just would not stay buttoned and his straight black tie had a deplorable habit of creeping over to the right or left shoulder and hanging there cheerfully through the entire course of a sermon. The listeners usually forgot within five minutes the unbuttoned vest and the tie askew. They were hearing a master engaged in the supreme art of interpreting Christ, and clothes did not matter.

He had little time for recreation, but did manage to put in a few care free hours sometimes puttering around in a little wood-working shop which he had fitted up in the basement of his home. There is no evidence that he ever made anything worth preserving, but his little hobby helped him to relax, and his efforts enabled him to indulge in a practical way his incurable yen to create.

He lived for many years at Nyack within easy walking distance of The Missionary Training Institute. His days were usually spent in New York in his office, directing a thousand and one activities, ranging anywhere from the hiring of an assistant janitor to deciding the size of a native church building in China or the Congo. Always at night he would return to Nyack in time for a late supper (it *was* supper in the Simpson household). He was not a heavy eater, but liked his food tastily prepared. He drank no coffee, but could take on unlimited amounts of English tea. He was never a faddist. He had no religious scruples about food, but allowed his personal tastes and common sense to decide what he should eat. A trace of his Scottish origin may be glimpsed in this, that for breakfast every morning he enjoyed a big bowl of—yes, that's right—*oats!*

Around home he was quiet and preoccupied. It is said that he never raised his voice, but spoke habitually in a low, conciliatory tone. He was sparing of words, except when someone did some little act of kindness for him. Then he would overflow with expressions of gratitude. He seldom retired before one or two o'clock in the morning, the hours after supper being spent in his own room in prayer and study or in writing the numerous books and articles which came from his heart in a steady stream for half a lifetime.

"O Mrs. Simpson," said a friend one day, "I'm curious. Tell me why your bedspreads are spotted all over with ink." Mrs. Simpson had grown patient with the years. "It's the Doctor," she explained. "You see, he writes in bed, and sometimes he nods, and his pen falls onto the bedspread and leaves a spot."

He was always up the next morning bright and early and on his way to New York by the six o'clock train. How he managed on four hours' sleep is one of those minor mysteries we run into sometimes when we examine the lives of the world's great. We do not try to explain it.

Mr. Simpson had convictions about medicine, and never used remedies at any time after he had come out into the light of divine healing. He was wise enough to hold to his convictions as being personal matters between himself and God. He never tried to screw them down upon the consciences of others. He had no phobia concerning doctors as some of his followers have had. "If you cannot have faith for your healing," he used to tell inquirers, "then get the best physician you are able to afford." He occasionally let down the bars on remedies on one count—if the word remedy does indeed describe the lowly cough drop. He did carry cough drops with him sometimes to ease the troublesome tickle in his throat. Once when preaching in Carnegie Hall in Pittsburgh he reached into his pocket for his handkerchief and, along with the 'kerchief came out a handful of cough drops. They rattled like marbles all over the platform! Mr. Simpson accepted the situation with smiling gravity and came off without loss of face, no mean achievement when it is remembered that he constantly had following him hecklers who would have paid good money to prove that he was not living what he preached.

There is some difference of opinion on the question of whether or not Mr. Simpson had a sense of humor. The facts are probably that he did originally have a good fund of native humor, but that his rigorous Calvinistic upbringing either destroyed it or made him so ashamed of it that he never indulged it except when caught off guard. Certainly, he had nothing of the good-humored fun in him that Spurgeon had, or Luther or D. L. Moody, though he could laugh heartily in his weak moments. He was heard on at least one occasion roaring with laughter like any plebeian at the side splitting stories of the Episcopalian rector, Dr. Henry Wilson.

Once in the Gospel Tabernacle he was sitting with a number of other ministers listening to a sermon by his friend William T. MacArthur. Suddenly the audience broke out into gales of laughter. MacArthur waited for them to quiet down, but the volume of laughter grew and continued so long that he finally turned to ask Mr. Simpson, who was the chairman, to do something to restore order. He was further dismayed to see Simpson slumped down in a heap on his chair, rocking with uncontrollable mirth! Those who have heard Mr. MacArthur in his prime will easily find it in their hearts to forgive Mr. Simpson!

The office staff at Alliance headquarters knew the

privilege of working for a man who managed to act like a Christian all day long, who was thoughtful, fair, tolerant and quiet spoken; but they also knew the difficulty of working for a human dynamo who never knew his own strength, and who judged everybody by himself. Curiously enough Mr. Simpson did not always pick his help from among his own followers, but often had working for him Catholics, Jews, and persons of no faith whatsoever. He treated them all alike.

His extreme modesty led him to refuse the degree of Doctor of Divinity offered him by a southern college in recognition of his scholarship and outstanding accomplishments. His reason was simply that he did not want any honor "that would exalt him in any measure above the lowliest of his brethren." His friend, Rev. Kenneth Mackenzie, who was responsible for this story, seemed to feel that this was a mistake on Simpson's part. He believed that a degree might have given him certain useful prestige before a religious world which sets much store by such things. On that subject, I do not risk an opinion. But he could not escape a degree. The grateful Christian public, by a kind of spiritual instinct, conferred a degree upon him, which, in spite of his reluctance, he carried to the end of his days.

CHAPTER SEVENTEEN

"Hallelujah! I'm tired"

The rapid expansion of The Christian and Missionary Alliance laid upon Mr. Simpson an ever growing weight of toil and responsibility. Like David, he had around him his "mighty men" to whom he delegated much of the actual labor, but for all that the demands of the work required that he be constantly on the move. No one could quite take his place. He was not only the elected head of the corporation, he was also the spiritual father of the movement, and as such he carried every detail of the work on his own heart.

He was a prolific writer, producing more than seventy books, thousands of printed sermons, scores of songs, and literally uncounted thousands of magazine articles and editorials. He traveled constantly, appearing for at least a few days at most of the large conventions throughout the United States and Canada, often stopping a night or two enroute to fellowship with some other church or society, then racing back to his own pulpit or to his office to dig out from under a mountain of accumulated business before leaving again for some other part of the country.

He was the recognized head of The Missionary Training Institute, as well as of all other schools that sprang up within the Society during the years. He taught at the Institute, managed his secular business as best he could, presided at the Board meetings and keynoted almost every conference and Council as long as he was able.

Among other duties that devolved upon him was that of steering his Society through the dangerous places she encountered as the years went on. These were usually doctrinal, though they sometimes affected policy. No more distasteful job could have been found for one of his temperament. He hated controversy and shrank from polemics, but he recognized the necessity for fighting when the Lord was leading the battle.

Though admittedly a mystic and a dreamer Mr. Simpson had a salty common sense which served him as a constant guide and mentor. His glimpses of the glory did not inflame his judgment nor unfit him for cool thinking. Consequently the waves of extreme teaching and questionable practices which swept across the United States about the turn of the century did not upset him in the least nor serve to deflect him from the path of sound doctrine and sane practice.

His prophetic fervency and his prominence made him a natural magnet, not only for those of sober mind who honestly sought to follow the way of truth, but for a host of others as well who were anything but sober minded. Crackpots and fanatics made his life miserable. His very terminology was against him at times, serving to encour-

131

age those of extreme views who sought to capitalize on his popularity. Just as the Seventh Day Adventists tried to claim Moody because he observed Saturday as a day for rest in preparation for his heavy day on Sunday, so various extremists hailed Simpson and embarrassed him with their attention.

The Pentecostal movement which sprang up in the early part of the Twentieth Century gave him no end of trouble. Doctrinally they were very close to Simpson's own position, so close that they could quote him to support their teachings, conveniently forgetting that the one tenet which distinguished them from all other groups was the very one which he consistently rejected. They held that the baptism of the Spirit must always, without exception, be accompanied by the physical manifestation of supernatural tongues. This belief became with them such an overpowering thing that it absorbed their interests and determined the whole character of their meetings. Not to win men to Christ, but to lead believers into "their baptism," became the ruling passion of their lives. To achieve this end they would do anything, even going so far as to practice bodily manipulation upon seekers, hoping in this way to produce "tongues." This led to some sad and shameful demonstrations in some of their gatherings. From such crass manifestations the cultured heart of Simpson revolted.

Into the Gospel Tabernacle at the time of the "tongues" excitement would come troops of these over-heated souls, confidently believing that, as Aquila and Priscilla had brought the mighty orator Apollos into clearer light, they were to be privileged to do the same thing for the great Dr. Simpson. But they never succeeded in ruffling the holy calm of the man. Under his keen eyes they felt themselves rather taken aback, and what had been planned as a concerted barrage usually fizzled off into a few sporadic amens, strangely meek and quiet for these people, and the service went on with a world of deep power, but with unimpeachable decorum. After a number of such attempts they finally gave up the struggle, though to his dying day they would come up every now and again with a report that at last Simpson had received his "baptism."

The simple fact is that Mr. Simpson was miles out ahead of these people in his spiritual experience. He did not need anything they had. He had found a blessed secret far above anything these perfervid seekers after wonders could ever think or conceive. There were many good people in the Pentecostal movement, and many admirable qualities about its adherents. Mr. Simpson did not want to pass judgment upon them till he had sufficient evidence, so he appointed Dr. Henry Wilson to visit Alliance, Ohio, a hot-bed of the new phenomenon, to study the meetings and report back. After a careful study Dr. Wilson made the following report, and it stands today as the crystallized utterance of the Society: "I am not able to approve the movement, though I am willing to concede that there is probably something of God in it somewhere."

When he felt the time was ripe, Simpson published a manifesto setting forth his position and renouncing the doctrine that all must speak in tongues. His utterance was kindly, but firm. From here on no one could doubt his stand. The result was that a number of prominent men withdrew from the Society and joined the new movement. In a few cities whole Alliance congregations went over to Pentecostalism, taking their church property with them. The grand total of churches going out in the general exodus was large, and the blow was hard for a young movement to bear. But the Society never forgot its early call. After a few uncomfortable years in which she was battered and bruised considerably by this controversy she shook off her aches and pains and launched forward stronger than ever in her initial task of world-evangelization.

Another question Mr. Simpson had to settle very early in the development of his Tabernacle and his missionary Society was whether divine healing was to be permitted to become an end in itself, or whether it was to be presented as a privilege which any child of God might enjoy, but which was not by any means central in the wide sweep of the gospel plan. Should healing or salvation take first place in the message of the Alliance?

John Alexander Dowie, a Scottish preacher who had come to the United States from Australia, forced the hand of Simpson and indirectly did him a great favor in compelling him to clear up the whole matter of divine healing as it related to himself and his Tabernacle. Dowie could see nothing but healing. He felt it to be of such supreme importance as to deserve his almost undivided attention. He proposed to Simpson that the two of them join forces and stump the country in the interest of divine healing. Mr. Simpson demurred. "No, Brother Dowie," said he, "I have four wheels on my chariot. I cannot agree to neglect the other three while I devote all my time to the one."

Impulsive and violent as he always was Dowie promptly turned against Simpson and set out with the express intention of discrediting him in the eyes of the public. He arranged throughout some of the principal cities of the United States a series of lectures in which he would tear Simpson to shreds and then tramp on the shreds! Simpson refused to fight back. Pittsburgh was the place chosen for the opening of the shredding campaign. Crowds filled the huge auditorium to hear the famous John Alexander Dowie. That evening, an hour or so before time for the opening lecture, Dowie was eating a fish dinner when a tiny bone became lodged cross-wise in his throat. The crowds waited, time went on and the speaker did not appear. He never showed up. It must have been an eloquent piece of bone, for it completely changed the plans of Mr. Dowie. He cancelled his series of lectures and crept back home to lick his wounds. When Simpson was informed of the turn things had taken, he said simply, "Oh, Dowie. Yes, I committed that man to God long ago."

Mr. Simpson was often made to suffer untold embarrassment through the honest but ill-advised, conduct of some of his followers. His missionary appeals were often so powerful that people came forward and laid valuable gifts on the altar to be converted into cash for the work of missions. This was wholly a voluntary act, no constraint or coercion being practiced upon the donors at any time. It was a beautiful expression of love as long as it remained free and spontaneous. But the head-long saints could not let well enough alone. They would make this

135

a law and bind it upon the consciences of the people. Many of them refused to wear on their persons anything more valuable than iron, and soon the inevitable button appeared bearing the words, "Gold for Iron," and every good consecrated soul was sure to be wearing one for the eyes of all to see. The men bought iron watch cases and the women substituted iron for gold on their clothing.

At the large conventions baskets were filled to overflowing with watches, rings and other ornaments which were donated to the cause of missions. Many a man not himself particularly interested in the Lord's work was known to blow up with a resounding echo when his wife came home from an Alliance Convention stripped of every valuable thing she possessed including the ring he had given her at the altar! The newspapers fastened on this with eager delight. It was right down their avenue, and they made the most of it. Hypnotism was just then becoming popular with the masses and this new pseudo-science served as a cue to the phenomenon. Mr. Simpson was a hypnotist practicing his art upon his audience to extract money from them for his own uses! Huge vats of printer's ink boiled and bubbled up and down the country, and there "was a deal of throwing about of brains," and then it all suddenly ceased. Reporters found something else to amuse them, and Simpson was forgotten.

Mr. Simpson was bothered by this outburst. The whole "gold for iron" fad had about it a slightly disquieting savor, and he wanted to keep his movement wholesome and free from taint. So he took steps to discourage the idea, and little by little the excitement died away.

Iron slowly disappeared from the ranks of the faithful and the girls got their wedding rings back. But for a long time after that the faces of some of the leading Alliance men would turn a bright red when the subject was brought up.

These are some of the problems with which Mr. Simpson had to wrestle as his work grew in scope and power. And he was not built for this kind of thing. It irked him and wearied his spirit and made him old before his time.

In the midst of all his numerous activities, Mr. Simpson somehow managed to find time to make several trips abroad. When a young minister of the Presbyterian church he had visited England. In the year 1885 he again visited London. In 1893 he made his longest journey, leaving New York in January and returning to the United States seven months later, after having completely circumnavigated the globe. On this journey he touched most of the Alliance mission fields, including the Holy Land, India, China and Japan.

In 1910 he visited South America. This journey proved very wearing upon his strength. When returning through Panama he became ill with a tropical fever. He recovered after a while, and managed to spiritualize everything as usual. He claimed that his experience helped him to sympathize more fully with the sufferings and trials of the workers on the fields! His last trip abroad was made in 1911 when he was 68 years of age. He went to the British Isles to fulfill a series of speaking engagements arranged for him by Pastor F. E. Marsh, of Bristol, England.

How he managed to pack into one lifetime all these manifold activities is his secret and God's. I do not pretend to know. And for all those years he never rested, had scarcely a day to himself. Vacations were unknown to him. Once he tried to take a few days away from his work but became so restless that he finally gave up the attempt and hurried back to his office to recover from the strain! He had to be doing something. Had he nursed himself along a bit more carefully he might have lasted a few years longer than he did. But who would have wanted it that way? Certainly not he. He must live his life after the pattern shown him in the mount. If he overworked it was for the love of God and men. If that is a fault it is not a common one.

The years after seventy were tired years for him. For the next four years he was as active as ever, but there came into his eyes and upon his frame more than a suggestion of deep fatigue. He had done five men's work, and he was feeling the weariness of five men. Nature had been good to him, and God had been better, but there is a limit to all things human.

In one of the early issues of *The Word, Work and World* Mr. Simpson tells about a thirteen-year-old Sudanese Christian girl who was compelled to carry a heavy load on her head for three days straight with hardly any time for rest between treks. She became pitifully weary, but, being a Christian, she would not complain. She felt she must continue to praise the Lord no matter how tired she was. At last she could take it no longer. Down she sank in a discouraged heap, burst into tears and wailed, "Hallelujah, I'm tired."

138

A. B. Simpson was tired. But he would not complain. His heart was still dancing before the ark though his body would not respond as gracefully as it had done in his younger yesterdays.

CHAPTER EIGHTEEN

Sundown

Over a period of about two years preceding his death Mr. Simpson's activities tapered off by degrees and his hold upon his work relaxed slowly. It was good that it was so, and providential. Had he fallen unexpectedly in his full strength, he might have left the work with no one to carry on. As it was, the shift from his shoulders to those of younger, stronger men was gradual. The transition from his leadership to that of the men who succeeded him was accomplished naturally and without a jar.

As his strength declined he turned over more and more of his duties to the men whom he affectionately called his "brethren." They took from his heart the burden of business cares that had harassed his soul for so long. His assistants filled the pulpit at the Tabernacle, and subordinate officers began to preside at the various official meetings of the Society. Simpson sat and watched with patriarchal calm the deliberations of the body he had led so brilliantly for over a quarter of a century. The people became used to seeing someone else in the chair. Mr. Simpson was getting ready to go away, and his "brethren" would have to learn to get along without him.

When the poet Longfellow lay in his casket, among others who came to pay their respects was the aged American essayist, Ralph Waldo Emerson. He walked into the room with that air of serenity which always characterized him, gazed down for a moment upon the face of his friend, and then said reverently, "I do not recall who it is that lies there, but he was a beautiful soul." A shadow had fallen across his mind, a mind among the most brilliant which the New World has ever produced.

Something like this also was experienced by Mr. Simpson in his last days. His exhausted brain refused to maintain its wonted thought patterns. He seemed to be living "out of the body" a large part of the time, becoming more and more absent-minded as the months wore on. He would greet his friends with warm cordiality, but they felt that he did not know always just who they were.

For a little time he went under a spiritual cloud also. He felt that the face of the Lord was hidden from him, and he mourned as one who had suffered the loss of his last and dearest treasure. It was then that he felt the need of his "brethren," and they stood by him loyally, tenderly, in the hour of his sorrow. One after another of the men who had been his friends through the years, missionaries, preachers, came to kneel beside his bed while he tried to sleep, or to walk arm in arm with him along the winding paths near his home. After a few weeks of this he recovered again the lost sense of the presence of the Well Beloved, and his happiness was child-like and full. After that there were no more spiritual shadows, only the dimness of a mind burnt out by a lifetime of unremitting toil.

While his body was weak and his mind clouded his affectionate heart continued to overflow like a fountain. The two-year-old daughter of a missionary who stayed for a time in his home was the particular object of his affection. The mother tells how Mr. Simpson used to draw the baby up to him and, because he could no longer see clearly, feel her soft little face and smile tenderly. Ministers and other Christian workers would come to visit him that he might lay his hands upon their head and pray. And they went away feeling that they had been in the presence of God.

In the spring of the year 1919 he suffered a slight stroke of paralysis. He recovered from this sufficiently that for the rest of the summer he was able to be around the house freely and to see friends occasionally. On Tuesday, October 28, while sitting on his front porch, and just after engaging in a long season of prayer for all his missionaries he went suddenly into a profound state of coma, from which he never rallied. His family watched by his bed till the next morning, when the labored breathing ceased and the weary frame rested at last.

After that he slept—the deep, honest sleep of one whose life of toil had earned him the right to sleep. Margaret, his wife, lingered a few years to walk about and cherish memories and dream again the hours she had never fully treasured while they were hers to enjoy. Not till he was gone did she know how much he had absorbed her life. She never quite lived again after he had left her. Often she would point out to some visiting friend

142

the places about the home that had been made sacred by his presence. "There on that chair he sat—on that path there by the rose bush he walked sometimes when he was tired and could not go further—by that arbor he stood in the twilight only an evening or two before he went away." She never bothered to explain who "he" might be. It never occurred to her that anyone could ask.

Just before it reaches Nyack the mighty Hudson, moving in slow majesty down to mingle with the sea, becomes prematurely ambitious and swells out to many times its normal width. The broad expanse of water that results men call the Tappan Zee. Across that blue bulge the sun will sometimes of a summer morning paint a streak of blazing scarlet as it rises in fire out of the hills above Tarrytown, and on many a clear winter night the watcher, gazing down, may see the sharp outline of a river steamer rippling the pale gold of the water as it creeps across the pathway of the moon. Half way up the towering hill that slopes westward from the river they laid Albert Simpson to rest.

And so he sleeps among the tall old trees that nod and sway above the lazy sprawling little village of Nyack. Along the path that runs near his grave, each day of the school year the students pass on their way to the classrooms, or it may be to sing and pray at the chapel service. He rests well there and the tramp of feet does not disturb his slumber. The education of Christian youth had been one of the dearest labors of his life. The cheerful shouts of the young people on the sloping campus of The Missionary Training Institute would be grateful music to his ears could he but hear them now.